What Everyone Is Looking For.
What Anyone Can Find.

As I look back, I realize that my life has been one of intense seeking without knowing what it was I was looking for. At times I sought after such things as health, self-esteem, money, material possessions, prestige, social status, professional recognition, security for the future, and friends I could trust and love. Despite my success in pursuing most of these, I never experienced the happiness they were supposed to bring.

It never occurred to me that I had the wrong goal, and that by searching for happiness outside myself, I was looking in the wrong place. Little did I realize that the love, joy, and peace of mind that I was looking for outside myself were already bountiful within me. They were simply blocked from my awareness by the fear that I alone had manufactured.

—from the Introduction

Books by Gerald G. Jampolsky, M.D.

Love Is Letting Go of Fear
Teach Only Love
Good-bye to Guilt

GOOD-BYE TO GUILT

Releasing Fear
Through Forgiveness

by

GERALD G. JAMPOLSKY, M.D.

with Patricia Hopkins
and William N. Thetford, Ph.D.

Foreword by John Denver

BANTAM BOOKS
TORONTO • NEW YORK • LONDON • SYDNEY • AUCKLAND

This book is dedicated to the innocent child who is ever present in all of us, and especially to those in my life I thought were my enemies through the projection of my own guilt onto them. I am most grateful to have come to recognize them as my sisters and brothers in light, through choosing to see them as my teachers of forgiveness.

Bantam Books are published by Bantam Books, Inc. Its trademark, consisting of the words "Bantam Books" and the portrayal of a rooster, is Registered in the United States Patent and Trademark Office and in other countries. Marca Registrada. Bantam Books, Inc. 666 Fifth Avenue, New York, New York 10103.

Contents

Foreword by John Denver   vii
Acknowledgments   x

PART I

Introduction   2
CHAPTER 1:   *Overview*   9
CHAPTER 2:   *What I Used to Believe*   15
CHAPTER 3:   *Easing God Out: The Ego and Its Belief*
             System   20
CHAPTER 4:   *The Ego's Attraction to Guilt*   29
CHAPTER 5:   *Love's Belief System*   37
CHAPTER 6:   *Love Is Listening*   51
CHAPTER 7:   *A Bridge to Heaven on Earth*   69

PART II

Introduction   80
LESSON   1:   *Forgiveness Heals and Ends the Game*
             of Guilt   82
LESSON   2:   *Choosing Love Offers Me Freedom*
             from Fear   92

LESSON 3:   *I Will Not Hurt Myself Again Today*   101
LESSON 4:   *Let Me Not See Myself As Limited*   110
LESSON 5:   *Let Peace Replace All My Fear*
            Thoughts Today   120
LESSON 6:   *Through Healed Vision I Know There*
            Is No Death   130
LESSON 7:   *Giving Love Away Is How I Keep It*   139
LESSON 8:   *Forgiveness Releases Me from My Past*   147
LESSON 9:   *I Can Know Love Only in the Present*   156
LESSON 10: *Without the Past I Claim My Freedom*
            Now   165
LESSON 11: *Only My Condemnation Injures Me*   175
LESSON 12: *I Will Receive What I Am Giving Now*   185
LESSON 13: *Forgiveness Offers Everything I Want*   195
LESSON 14: *In My Defenselessness My Safety Lies*   204

Epilogue   213

Foreword

What I most appreciate about Jerry Jampolsky is his ability to articulate emotions and describe experiences that all of us have had, in a way that allows us to understand our own problems, to make clearer who and what we are as human beings and what makes us tick. He helps us to begin to know why we do some of the things we do. When I read Jerry's words or talk with him, I am constantly reminded of how I related to certain troubling feelings or relationships in my own life, and I find myself saying, "Oh, I see, that's what was going on."

I, too, am a student of *A Course in Miracles*. I have read Jerry's books *Love Is Letting Go of Fear* and *Teach Only Love*, and now this manuscript of *Good-bye to Guilt*. These books have been invaluable to me, not only in understanding myself but in organizing and articulating my thoughts about life and the world we live in to others. Most importantly, Jerry supports and strengthens my concept of where the human race is going, and how it will get there—how we can create the world of peace, a dream we all have.

In the recent "Me Decade" there were myriad programs, training centers, workshops, and seminars, which allowed us to focus on ourselves as individuals, and to use self-awareness and self-expression as tools for self-help and the expansion of consciousness. For many, myself included, it was also a step toward spiritual growth and understanding. What was rarely, if ever, included in the descriptions, analyses, and criticisms of the "Me Decade" was its possible impact on the world we live in and its potential for affecting society as a whole.

Many of us have wished that the world were different and wondered aloud about how we could change it and make it a better place for everyone to live in. I am one who believes that we cannot change the world, but that we can only change ourselves, and in the process, the world will be different. I truly believe that we can create a new and better world.

A Course in Miracles tells us that "you cannot change your mind by changing your behavior . . . but that you *can* change your mind." And when someone truly changes his mind, "he has changed the most powerful device that was ever given him for change."

Our world is one of conflict and separation. It is a world of judgment and punishment, where others are responsible for our problems. It is an unstable world. As we learn about guilt and fear, and the power they exercise in our lives and relationships, their effect on society and the world as a whole becomes clear. As we begin to understand the power of love and forgiveness, it becomes easier and easier to choose the environment in which we wish to exist. By making the conscious choice, we find that the space in which we live is different; we begin to experience the peace of mind and fullness of heart that is the gift of a loving God.

I know that the thousands all over the world who love Jerry and whose lives have been enhanced by his message are eagerly looking forward to this new book. They have a treat in store. In clear and beautiful prose Jerry tells us that peace is a conscious choice. Saying good-bye to guilt is a vital step in making that choice.

JOHN DENVER
Windstar
Aspen, Colorado
November 1984

Acknowledgments

I would like to thank the many readers who wrote to Patricia Hopkins and me expressing the wish that the articles we wrote for *Unity* magazine be made into a book. This book is an expansion and modification of those articles.

I wish to express my heartfelt thanks to Mary Abney for her continued loving support and patience, and for the many hours of typing that preceded the publication of this book. I am also grateful to Grace Bechtold, senior editor, Bantam Books, Inc., for her continued support and encouragement.

The quotations that appear before each chapter and each lesson are from *A Course in Miracles*, published in 1975 by the Foundation for Inner Peace (P.O. Box 635, Tiburon, CA 94920), and are reprinted here with the permission of the publisher. I am indebted to Judy and Bob Skutch for their permission to quote so generously from this material.

PART I

Introduction

I believe the most important issue that all of us face in our lives is healing relationships. The purpose of this book is to show how relationships can be healed through forgiveness by saying "good-bye to guilt" and letting go of the fear and blame that keep us separate from each other.

Very simply, guilt can be defined as the feeling of self-condemnation that we experience after we do something we think is wrong. And fear can be thought of as our feelings of anxiety or agitation when we perceive danger—in any form. In the context of this book, guilt and fear are closely related and frequently synonymous. Forgiveness means letting go of the past. Unless we forgive others for what we think they have done to us, we will be unable to forgive ourselves and experience peace of mind.

For most of my life, without fully recognizing it, I've had expectations that I wanted other people to fulfill. I wanted them to fit into a mold of my making. In a sense, I was saying that the world would be a wonderful place if everyone would just do things my way. If they did things my way, they became my friends, and if they did not measure up to my expectations, I no longer wished to have them around.

The way I looked at things, it was always the other person who had to change if our relationship was to be healed—never me. Indeed, it has been quite astonishing for me to learn that it is only my mind that needs healing, and that to heal a relationship, all I have to do is release my guilt and fear from the past through forgiveness.

As I began to look at the unhealed relationships in my life and to explore why they did not work, the word "seeker" came to mind. I believe that most of us can be described as seekers. In my late fifties, as I look back, I realize that my life has been one of intense seeking without knowing what it was I was looking for. At times I sought after such things as health, self-esteem, money, material possessions, prestige, social status, professional recognition, security for the future, and friends I could trust and love. Despite my success in pursuing most of these, I never experienced the happiness they were supposed to bring.

It never occurred to me that I had the wrong goal, and that by searching for happiness outside myself, I was looking in the wrong place. I had absolutely no conscious awareness that I was suffering from a self-imposed state of spiritual deprivation, that I was starving myself and suffering from spiritual hunger and thirst. (I recognize now that the condition of spiritual deprivation is not unique to me, and that everyone seeks for something constant and everlasting that can be found within.) Little did I realize that the love, joy, and peace of mind that I was looking for outside myself were already bountiful within me. They were simply blocked from my awareness by the fear that I alone had manufactured. It never occurred to me that I had become afraid of love. Rather, I had convinced myself that I was unworthy of love, unlovable, and destined to be alone and separate.

I began to change my way of looking at the world in 1975. Until then I had considered myself a militant atheist, and the last thing I was consciously interested in was being on a spiritual pathway that would lead to God. In that year I was introduced to a set of three books, a self-taught course in spiritual transformation, titled *A Course in Miracles*.*

My resistance was immediate. I did not like the title, and I found the size and weight (three pounds) of the books both discouraging and threatening. Nevertheless, after reading just one page, I had a sudden and dramatic experience. There was an instantaneous memory of God, a feeling of oneness with everyone in the world, and the belief that my only function on earth was to serve God.

Because of my Jewish background, however, I found that as I got into the course, I developed a great deal of resistance to its Christian terminology. Since I had been an atheist for most of my life, the word "God" was troublesome to me. I protected myself from the fear and anxiety caused by the spiritual terminology by translating it in my own mind to "higher state of consciousness."

It has been an exciting experience for me at long last to begin to say good-bye to guilt and fear by learning how to apply the principles in *A Course in Miracles* in very practical ways in every part of my life.

Although the course will be discussed more fully in Chapter 1, I would like to mention a few of its fundamental concepts here. One of its basic tenets is that we can experience only two emotions: love, which is our natural inheritance, and fear-guilt, which our mind has invented. (In the course, as well as in this book, "fear" and "guilt" are regarded as negative twins that feed upon each other. Although both words are used throughout the book, the relationship between guilt and fear is symbiotic: one can-

A Course in Miracles (The Foundation for Inner Peace, 1975).

not exist without the other. Guilt reinforces fear, as fear reinforces guilt, in a seemingly endless cycle.) It is the goal of the course, and also of this book, to help us choose which emotion we want to experience. Rather than perceiving people as attacking us, we are encouraged to experience love by choosing to see others as loving, or by giving a call of help for love.

As I have continued to travel on my spiritual journey, it has become more clear to me than ever before that there are many different pathways to God, and *A Course in Miracles* as a tool for spiritual growth is simply the way I have chosen for myself. Although its principles emphasize that love and forgiveness are universal, the course is clearly not meant—nor would it be suitable—for all.

The three key concepts of this book, and of the course that it is based on, are that relationships can be healed

1. when we let go of guilt and fear through forgiveness,

2. when we have peace of mind as our only goal, and

3. when we learn to listen to our inner voice as a guide for directions and decision-making.

Since becoming a traveler on the spiritual pathway in 1975, I am frequently asked to contrast myself now with the person I was then. It is not easy for me to do this without reinforcing the distortions of my ego. However, I would say that although I still get angry, depressed, and have feelings of futility and hopelessness, I do not hang on to these feelings for the interminable periods of time that I used to. I now seem to be able to take responsibility more frequently for what I see and experience, and I no longer see value in suffering and pain.

The greatest obstacle that I have, and that I suspect most

people have when they become more spiritually alive, is that I have a personality-self, an ego, which wants to control, predict, and be in charge. It is an ego that doesn't want to relinquish itself, and that sees peace of God as its enemy and conflict as its friend.

Yet I find, more and more, that I am content with just being, rather than interpreting the behavior of myself and others. More and more, the purpose of joining with everyone I meet has become my goal. More and more, I see the importance of being still, of giving all my needs to the voice of love within me, and experiencing the peace and love of God.

I am now more willing to choose peace rather than conflict. When I forget these principles and get off the track, I find it helpful to remember that my own ego may be compared to a TV series that continues to rerun old movies. We have seen them before, we know how they begin and end, and yet our ego tries to create the illusion that they are brand new.

These shows frequently tell stories about unmet needs from our past and fantasized desires of the future. They keep us so preoccupied with the past and future that we are unable to awaken from our sleepy dream-state and experience the joy that it is possible to find in the present moment.

The TV script is one that our ego has written, produced, directed, and starred in; it then disassociates itself from all of these roles. Scenes of attack, murder, and violence of all kinds appear on the screen, but our ego would have us believe that we are merely passive observers of this violence and not the authors of it.

Healing relationships is about learning how to stop the horror shows in our minds that seem so real. In this book I have made an effort to share with you what I have learned along the spiritual path, as well as the people I have met who have become my teachers.

Part I deals with the basic spiritual principles that we can use to find another way of looking at the world. Part II has to do with how these lessons can be applied. It consists of my discussing as simply as I can a spiritual principle and then sharing one or more examples of its practical applications.

Let us remind ourselves and each other that relationships become healed as we let forgiveness erase all of our guilty, fearful feelings and thoughts of separateness. And as we travel together in this book and in life, let us be witnesses to each other in learning to say "good-bye to guilt" and awaken to the presence of God's love and our natural state of happiness—and acknowledge that we are all gifts of love to each other and ourselves.

"The guiltless have no fear,
for they are safe and
recognize their safety."

CHAPTER ONE

Overview

I would like to share with you a brief overview of the philosophy of *A Course in Miracles* on which this book is based. *A Course in Miracles* is a self-study program for personal and spiritual transformation that emphasizes the necessity of relying on our own internal teacher for guidance rather than looking for teachers outside ourselves. It consists of a text, which sets forth the concepts on which its thought system is based; a workbook for students containing 365 lessons (one for each day of the year), designed for practical application of the course's principles to daily life; and a manual for teachers written in question and answer form to clarify terms and issues related to the course.

The course is a spiritual teaching, not a religion. It uses Christian terminology, but it is ecumenical in nature. The course states that "a universal theology is impossible, but a universal experience is not only possible but necessary." Its emphasis is on application, and, after studying the course, students are encouraged to demonstrate and live the spiritual principles of forgiveness and giving through love in their daily lives.

The goal of the course is to lead us from the world of the ego—our body/personality-self—to the world of love. Once we are caught in the world of the ego, which is the world of perception, it is as though we are imprisoned in a dream. We need help to awaken from this dream since what our senses reveal to us merely reinforces our belief in the reality of the dream. The course stresses that as long as we identify with our ego or body/personality-self and believe we are limited by the boundaries of what we perceive in the physical world, we cannot experience our true reality—our spiritual self.

Until we challenge the reality of our ego, we will continue to go through life more concerned with getting than giving, feeling guilty, separate, and afraid. We will make condemning judgments, blaming ourselves and others. With the ego as our guide, guilt and fear will rule our lives; conflict will never totally disappear, and we can anticipate that our "reality" will be destroyed by sickness and death.

If we are willing to detach from our ego, it is then possible to correct our perceptions. The world of corrected perception is the world of love. It is a world that is seen through the filter of spiritual vision, the vision of love, rather than through the distortions of our ego.

Like a cloud obscuring the sun, the guilt and fear that we carry within us block our ability to experience the presence of love, which has never left us. We are all miracles of love, but we are blind to that truth. A miracle can be thought of as a shift in perception that removes the fear and guilt that block our awareness of love's presence, which is our reality.

I would like to share with you some quotations from the course that are the underlying themes—or heartbeats—of the philosophy expressed in this book.

"When you feel guilty your ego is in command, because only the ego can experience guilt."

"Only your mind can produce fear."

"I can be hurt by nothing but my thoughts."

"Love holds no grievances."

"I will not be afraid of love today."

"Love and guilt cannot coexist, and to accept one is to deny the other."

"To love yourself is to heal yourself."

"All healing is release from the past."

"Forgiveness is my function as the light of the world."

"Only my own condemnation injures me. Only my own forgiveness sets me free."

"Forgiveness ends the dream of conflict here."

Attitudinal Healing

Because of the profound effect the course had on my life, I decided to apply its principles in working with catastrophically ill children. In 1975, my inner guidance led me to help establish The Center for Attitudinal Healing in Tiburon, California, to fulfill that function.*

*The course itself is not used at the center, nor is anyone connected with the center required to study it. There is, however, the expectation that the staff adopt and demonstrate the principles of attitudinal healing, which represent universal, nonsectarian, spiritual truths.

At the time I helped found the center, I equated the death of my body with the end of life, and I had terrible hang-ups about the inevitability of my own death. Working with children and adults who were facing the possibility of their own deaths, and seeing them and the members of their extended families as my teachers, gave me a wonderful opportunity to heal my own attitudes about death.

In addition to groups for catastrophically ill children and adults, we have recently begun a program for children whose parents have life-threatening illnesses. I would like to emphasize, however, that the center's programs are not limited to those with life-threatening illnesses. We also have a person-to-person program where people come together for only two reasons: to learn how to let go of judgments, and to practice forgiveness. The concepts used at the center have wide, practical applications, and we have been invited to introduce these principles of attitudinal healing to retirement centers, educational and medical institutions, businesses, and governmental agencies.

Our center offers no treatment: it is an educational center that serves as a supplement to the medical model. Our definition of health is inner peace, and we define healing as letting go of fear. We believe that it is not people or conditions in our external world that cause us to be upset, but rather the thoughts and attitudes we have about people and conditions that cause us to be in conflict and distress.

Letting go of our past thoughts of guilt, fear, and condemning judgments is what we call "attitudinal healing." Attitudinal healing is concerned only with changing the thoughts in our own mind. It is not focused on changing situations or other people in our lives.

We do our best at the center to establish an atmosphere of unconditional love where we learn to recognize the love in others rather than concentrate on their faults. It is our belief that giving and receiving are the same, and, therefore, by helping others we help ourselves. This principle implies that there is no separation—that our minds are joined. We emphasize that the present moment is the only time there is, and its only purpose is for giving love and letting go of the negative thoughts from our past. At our center, everyone is regarded as both a teacher and a learner.

There are now approximately thirty-five centers in the United States and in other parts of the world. Perhaps the greatest gift we have been given, which is the basis for attitudinal healing, is the power that comes from knowing that we are free to choose the thoughts we put in our minds, and that by changing these thoughts, we can change our experience.

We do not have to have a life-threatening illness to apply these principles in our daily lives. All of us have unhealed relationships that can be healed, and we can free ourselves from our bondage to the past by becoming aware of the boundless love within us. It is this bondage and attachment to our guilt and fears of the past that cause not only our internal conflict, but the external conflicts we see in the world. It is so easy for all of us to become stuck in the mundane issues and self-pleasures of our lives—and to forget that PEACE . . . PEACE . . . PEACE in the world is truly the number one issue of our lives.

The premise of this book is that to heal our relationships we must first be willing to find peace within ourselves and then extend that peace to everyone. As each of us makes the healing of our relationships through love and forgiveness the most important thing we can do in our lives, peace in the world will become inevitable.

*"You can hold on to the past
only through guilt."*

CHAPTER TWO

What I Used to Believe

My old perception of the world was that it was out to get me—to do me in. My parents were always reminding me to hurry, hurry, hurry, no matter what I was doing. As an adult, I continued to hurry through life without being clear whether I was running away from something or toward something.

As I look back on my life, I am convinced that I have spent most of my time doing battle with myself or trying to run away from myself. As a child, I was clumsy, hyperactive, and had tremendous problems learning how to read and write. When it came to school, I was never able to please my teachers or my parents; I felt I was a loser. My message to the world and to myself was, "I can never do anything right." And in a world where the love you received depended on how well you performed, not being right meant to me that I was unlovable, and it was unlikely that I would ever be loved.

I discovered, however, that I could make others right by becoming more guilty. The more guilty I became, the better they liked it. Becoming guilty became a way of pleasing others. Consequently, I became a storehouse of guilt, and the storehouse expanded and grew beyond anything I could possibly imagine.

Since I believed I was a second-class citizen, I concentrated on being a first-class pessimist—at least that was something I felt I could control. I decided to fulfill the negative expectations others had of me by doing things to make myself wrong in order to make them right. It gave me a crazy sense of power finally to be right about something. Although I couldn't succeed at making people love me, I became an expert at making people angry. By provoking anger, I reinforced my belief that I could control something by demonstrating convincingly what an unworthy and unloving person I was.

I experienced the world as a precarious place where I might be attacked at any moment. This fearful child complex remained with me into adulthood. Through most of my adult life I continued to be fearful of being attacked, rejected, and unloved.

I developed all kinds of other fears besides: fear of death, fear of life, fear of love, fear of having fun and being happy, fear of success and fear of failure, fear of closeness in any relationship, fear of not trusting myself or others. In addition, I acquired certain phobias, such as fear of high places and water.

I learned how to wear a multitude of costumes to hide my true feelings. I used these costumes to prevent people from getting close to me, and to manipulate and control others, even when it was clearly against my own well-being to do so. I was afraid I would be destroyed if I removed my masks and showed people who I really was. As a result, I became very competitive—striving to get more and more, but also living in fear of losing what I already had.

The world became an increasingly frightening place for

me. However, I hung on by my fingernails hoping to find some moments of pleasure to offset the endless hours of insecurity and pain. Even though I adapted as best I could, I always felt that the worst was yet to come. I was in a perpetual state of conflict, both fearing death and wishing it would come and rescue me.

While at the time I was sure my feelings were unique, I am now convinced that everyone is familiar with all of these emotions to some degree. It is only their form and intensity that seem to be different for each of us.

What I have been describing is a world based on fear and guilt. It is a depressing world where we believe that sooner or later bad things are bound to happen to us, and our unhappy experiences from the past will repeat themselves in the future. It is a world in which relationships are often troubled and short-lived, and the way we handle disharmony in our relationships is to get out of them. It is a world that believes in judgment, unforgiveness, and punishment; a world in which others are seen as guilty and responsible for our problems.

It is an unstable world, terminally ill from lack of love, in which we frequently feel helpless, a world we seem hell-bent on destroying. It is a world that doesn't know the meaning of consistent peace, a world in which we live with the threatening knowledge that one person can press a button and annihilate us all.

What I used to believe seemed very real to me, and there didn't seem to be any other way of looking at the world. It was not until I began to be on a spiritual pathway that I began to consider the idea, as many have before me, that there are two ways of looking at the world, and each of these requires a totally different belief system. These belief or thought systems are based on different ways of looking at cause and effect, truth and illusion, life and death.

The commonly shared thought system of the world is the thought system of the ego. It is based on perceiving a world of separation, guilt, fear, attack, and unhealed relationships. It is a world of misperception.

The opposite of this belief system is the thought system of love, which is based on perceiving a world of unity, a world of unconditional love, peace, and happiness, and a world where relationships are healed. It is a world based on God's love—a world in which perception has been corrected through forgiveness.

At the superficial level of awareness, there may be a great temptation for the majority of us to think that the belief system of love is a simplistic pipe dream. In contrast, the ego's belief system seems to be what the real world we live in is all about. Most of us would be threatened by any suggestions that we would be better off if we changed our beliefs, and we would actively resist doing so.

May I suggest that before you read the remainder of this chapter and the next four chapters in which these two systems will be contrasted, you allow your mind to be still for just a few minutes. Try to let go of all things you thought you knew, all thoughts about what is real and what is not, about who you are and what you are doing here, and all the values you hold dear to your heart whether they be good or bad. Would you now have a little willingness and open-mindedness, not necessarily to believe, but just to consider another possibility? That perhaps the way we have been looking at the world is simply a dream that we have invented in order to shut out the memory of love and a loving God?

*"For the ego really believes that it can get and keep **by making guilty**."*

CHAPTER THREE

Easing
God
Out:
The Ego and Its
Belief System

L et us consider the following possibilty: We invented
the ego's belief system out of fear and guilt engendered
by the mistaken belief that we have made ourselves separate from God. The ego is a symbol of our belief in this
separation. While separation from God is clearly impossible, through the eyes of the ego we believe this is true and
that God is out to punish us for our "guilty" deeds.

The purpose of the ego's thought system is to hide the
memory of God from our awareness by reinforcing our
feelings of guilt and fear. It can accomplish this only by
destroying the reality of love and substituting the illusion
of guilt in its place. Since the opposite of love is fear, the
ego's existence depends on our continuing belief in the reality of guilt and punishment, and the acceptance of its
goals of conflict, war, and death.

The Ego vs. God

The ego's attitude toward God is inconsistent. At times it views God as some supernatural, external being beyond our comprehension that loves and rewards us if we are good, and punishes us if we are bad and have sinned. At other times it is ambivalent about whether or not God even exists, and sometimes it rejects the idea of God altogether. The ego is threatened by God and continues to do its best to ease God out of our lives.

A beautiful example of our ambivalent feelings about God is described in Alice Walker's book, *The Color Purple*. Two women are having a discussion about God and one of them says, "But it ain't easy, trying to do without God. Even if you know he ain't there, trying to do without him is a strain."

I sometimes think that I, and many others, have gone through life feeling guilty for the wrongs I think I have committed, feeling distrustful of myself and others, and wondering in what way I am going to be punished next. Because many of us have had painful life experiences in which we did not think our religious training and belief in God helped, we have ended up turning away from both.

The ego can be defined as our body/personality or lower self. It is the part of our mind that is split off or separated from our spiritual mind, which contains only God's loving thoughts. This split in our mind can be thought of as illusory; it can be contrasted to our true mind, a mind filled with love that is indivisible.

The thought system of the ego is based on guilt and fear. Its motto is, "Seek but never find what you are looking for." It is preoccupied with condemning judgments, attack and defense thoughts and is a master of deception. Its goal is to control everything and to believe it is right all the

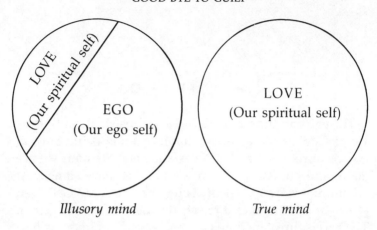

Illusory mind   *True mind*

time. It expends an enormous amount of energy trying to predict the future based on our past experiences. It would have us believe that our body/personality-self is the accidental result of a purposeless world, and that we are at the mercy of events and situations over which we have no control. Its foundation is built on doubts and uncertainties, so it is ambiguous and ambivalent about everything. It is characterized by complexity and confusion rather than simplicity.

The ego's world is a pleasure/pain world, and, for most of us, there is more pain than pleasure. It believes that if you don't fear the past and worry about the future, the world will fall apart. Separation is its game; so thinking of yourself first, getting and holding on to what little you can claim as your own, jealousy, possessiveness, and rejection are the core of its existence. The ego is certain that it—not God—is the director and ruler of the universe.

Ego Identification

Our identity as defined by our ego is limited to the five senses: hearing, seeing, touching, smelling, and tasting. It is based on the interpretation and evaluation of what these senses feed back to our brain. It is a limited identity based on experiences of the past extending into the present and projected into the future.

As the ego sees it, our identity is our body and our personality-self. Thus, my identity as Jerry Jampolsky becomes confined and limited to my body, mind, and brain, which are separate from everyone else's. Seen through the eyes of the ego, my identity is dependent on the opinions and judgments other people have about me, as well as the opinions and judgments I have about myself. My present identity is seen simply as an extension of my past.

The following poem which was sent to me recently by Saskia Davis looks at our identification with the ego in a lighthearted way:

THE COSMIC CHUCKLE

Just look at me,
The great chooser of LIFE!
What a funny thing I did!
I created me;
Fancied me up in human package
And delivered me to that
Most peculiar earth plane
(Which, by the way, I created too).

Now, there was I;
And what did I do?
I played a game.
Pretended I had no choice,
No power, no will.
Pretended I was weak
And separate from all the other parts of Me.
Pretended I depended
On weird little circumstances,
Just custom created
For the game I played.

And—the funniest thing that I did—
Well, (hee-hee, ho-ho, hee-hee)
I pretended I was not pretending.
I pretended so intensely.
I finally took me seriously.

Then, on and on I played,
Forgetting who I really was.
"Good" and "bad" I often judged,
And "right" and "wrong"
And "mine" and "thine."
Sometimes I made war against myself.
"There's not enough for me," I'd cry,
"So give me what is thine"

Oh, how serious I grew!
It all seemed so very real.
No power, no choice, no will,
Just weak and separate.
How exciting I thought it all!

The mystery of wondering
If maybe, just maybe,
Even by accident,
I could have some little desire of mine,
And that great charge of discouragement
That came over me as I realized that
By all the little rules,
Well, of course, there was no hope.

Oh, woe.

And the one great fear I had,
(How it delights me, looking back!)
It was of giving up that silly game,
For then, I feared, I'd cease to be.
I thought, (hee-hee, ho-ho, hee, hee)
I thought there'd be no more of me!

SASKIA DAVIS

What the Ego Sees As Truth

In the ego's thought system, truth changes constantly because it is always relative. What is true is whatever the majority of people believe to be correct at any given time.

For instance, ten years ago if a physician diagnosed someone as having chronic high blood pressure, the patient was told that he/she would have to take blood-pressure medication for the rest of his/her life. This was considered a medical fact, an indisputable truth.

With the advent of biofeedback technology came the knowledge that we can now learn to control our autonomic nervous system through an electrical feedback system and mental imagery. With the approval of their physicians, many people are finding they no longer have to take any blood-pressure medication. When people discover they can lower their own blood pressure, they also recognize that they can accept responsibility for their reactions to stress. This recognition often allows them to see that it is their own perception and interpretation of stress in the environment that caused their disorder in the first place.

These examples illustrate how changeable "truth" is when it depends on perceptions and interpretations that shift whenever new information becomes available.

Special Relationships/Conditional Love

The ego's thought system is most clearly seen in relationships that we regard as particularly close or special. These relationships are based on the belief that we lack something in ourselves which only other people can supply, and unless we get it from them, we will be incomplete and unhappy. Such special relationships are necessarily built on guilt and lack of trust. From the ego's viewpoint, other people exist to satisfy our needs, and, therefore, we are unable to see ourselves and others as we really are.

This mutual meeting of needs is what the ego calls "love." It is important to emphasize that this kind of "love" is always conditional and exclusive. Unlike unconditional love, which is inclusive and based on total acceptance of oneself and others, conditional love is always based on qualifications, reservations, and limitations. Most of what we call love in our lives is conditional love, which is founded on scarcity, on getting and giving to get, and on bargaining and trading.

The identifying word in conditional love is "if"—I will love you *if* you perform the way I want you to, *if* you fit into the mold I have developed in my mind for you. I will love you *if* you get better grades in school . . . *if* you come home from work on time . . . *if* you remember my birthday . . . *if* you demonstrate more affection and become a more assertive and energetic sexual partner to me . . . *if* you stop smoking . . . *if* you lose weight . . . *if* you stop complaining—an endless series of "ifs." If the other person gives us what we want, or changes to satisfy our needs, we feel happy. If the person doesn't give us what we want or make the changes we think are necessary, we feel irritated and frustrated. And when our irritations and frustrations intensify, they become anger and hatred.

Relationships founded on conditional love are really love/hate relationships. They are based on wanting something from the other person because of a mistaken feeling of scarcity and the belief that the other person has something we lack. In these love/hate relationships pain, fear, and instability are insured because of the feelings of jealousy, possessiveness, and competition that characterize conditional love. Conditional love relationships are exclusive relationships, which shut others out. The purpose of conditional love relationships is to place a limit on love by serving as a substitute for the inclusive love of God.

My dear friend and writer, Joan Walsh Anglund, recently wrote to me some of her thoughts on desire and its relationship to conditional love:

> *To the extent that we want*
> *something from someone,*
>
> *To that exact degree*
> *we will be in pain,*
>
> *For it is desire that*
> *brings pain*
>
> *And it is love that*
> *brings joy.*

*"While you feel guilty your ego
is in command, because only the
ego can experience guilt."*

CHAPTER FOUR

The Ego's Attraction
to Guilt

The ego's attraction to guilt cannot be fully understood unless we first discuss the nature of perception. For it is how we see the world around us that determines how we react to it. And it is our perceptions that tell us what we see, based on the interpretations and evaluations of what our senses report to us. Each of us sees the world differently, depending on our individual needs, wishes, past experiences, and present beliefs.

While we may think of our perceptions as photographs of things outside ourselves taken by a camera, they are really projections of thoughts that originate in our own minds. Since we always look in before we look out, what we see is our own state of mind reflected outward.

That perception is a choice (even though we may not be aware of making it) and not a fact is clearly demonstrated by the various interpretations people give of everyday events in their lives. If ten people witness an accident, for instance, it would be unusual for any two of them to agree on the details of how it occurred. Since our perceptions are fragmented, we see only bits and pieces of any situation— never the whole. What we believe to be the truth is simply our own interpretation and evaluation of what we perceive. Many of the difficulties and disagreements we have with other people are based on the highly individualized nature of our perceptions.

Decision-making

We cannot live in the world without making decisions, and in order to do so, we must listen and be directed by one of two voices: the voice of the ego, which speaks for our changeable perceptions, or the voice of love—the voice of God. Our ego mind has a continuum of mental pictures based on our past perceptions of guilt and fear that determines what we think we want in the present.

Our ego deceives us about the way in which we decide by persuading us that we are making brand new decisions each day based on what is occurring in the present moment. Its voice states, "I want what I want right now." However, on another level the voice of the ego says to us, "Hey, watch out, you are vulnerable, and all those hurtful experiences of the past are going to be repeated."

When we listen to the ego's voice, our decisions are frequently founded on judgments and interpretations of past experiences. To survive, the ego tells us we must look for guilt in others or in ourselves, and this preoccupation with who is guilty and who is innocent becomes the basis for our decision-making.

This attraction of the ego to guilt produces a corresponding fear of love since it is impossible for love and fear to coexist. The continuous search for guilt as a basis for making decisions leaves us feeling more and more fearful and devoid of love. With our ego-mind on automatic pilot, constantly superimposing the past on the present, it is no wonder our problems seem to defy lasting solutions.

Projection

When we perceive others through the eyes of guilt, we are likely to engage in projection. Projection is the mechanism by which we deny responsibility for and externalize a thought or feeling we are experiencing—such as guilt—by holding someone else responsible for it. This "someone" else can be our spouse, business partner, parent, child, our president, an internal revenue agent, or anyone who seems to play a role in our lives. We believe if only they would behave differently, then we would not experience the difficulties we are having.

For example, I remember when my two sons were in grammar school I tried, with no success, to make them feel guilty about their untidy rooms in an attempt to motivate them to change their behavior. As I look back on that situation, I can see that I denied my own guilt about having a very messy office by projecting the problem onto them. Projecting our problems onto others never solves the problem; it simply recycles the guilt.

Guilt

Guilt is the feeling of self-condemnation that we experience after we do something we think is wrong. It is impossible to experience feelings of guilt without also anticipating punishment of ourselves or, when the guilt is projected, the punishment of others. Although we may not be consciously aware of it, the underlying source of our basic guilt is always the belief that we have "sinned," and the fear that God will attack and punish us for our un-worthiness.

Guilt and fear cannot coexist with love. When we hold on to these negative feelings, we are prevented from experiencing the peace and presence of God.

It is a psychological fact that if we hold on to guilt, we will attempt to handle it either by attacking ourselves (frequently expressed as symptoms of depression or physical illness), or projecting the guilt onto someone else. The ego tries to conceal from us that when we take responsibility for our mistakes, they no longer call for guilt and punishment, but rather for release through correction. For example, if we feel we have offended people, we can correct our mistake by apologizing to them directly. Holding on to guilt, on the other hand, is the ego's way of keeping us trapped in the past by blaming ourselves or others.

The Game of "Who Is Guilty and Who Is Innocent"

The game of "Who is guilty and who is innocent" takes place in most marriages and other relationships as well. One person throws a "hot potato" of guilt to his spouse, partner, colleague, or friend. The other person has a choice of catching it and holding on to it, or throwing it back. More often than not, the other person throws it back, and this is the way the game of "Who is guilty and who is innocent" is played. The only way both parties can win is to stop playing the game. It is only when we no longer want to hold on to the "hot potato" of guilt and are willing to drop it, that we can then make room for love.

The Effects of Guilt

A few weeks ago I had a conversation with a close friend that replayed for me some unpleasant moments of guilt from my past. For the next twenty-four hours, I was so overwhelmed and paralyzed by these guilty memories that I felt as though I were under the influence of drugs.

The effects of guilt are, indeed, like taking too many sleeping pills or painkillers, or having too much alcohol or sun. I felt as though my brain and body were immobilized, and I was locked in a vise or confined in a prison cell with no hope of escape.

Holding on to guilt is guaranteed to

1. make us feel under attack;

2. justify our feelings of anger toward ourself or someone else;

3. destroy our self-esteem and confidence;

4. make us feel depressed, hollow, and empty;

5. destroy our sense of peace;

6. make us feel unloved.

It is not an exaggeration to see guilt as a self-made poison, which we administer to ourselves frequently. It is the most effective tool the ego has for insuring that we will remain hopelessly bound to our past and therefore not recognize each opportunity the present offers us for our release. There is only one known antidote for guilt: complete forgiveness, starting with ourself and extending to everyone who shares the world with us.

Forgiveness

The ego looks on forgiveness with a split mind; it counsels us to "forgive but don't forget." It is really a double message that says, "Don't forgive completely; don't forget the past or you will be vulnerable." Lack of forgiveness is the heartbeat of the ego. It continues to justify making condemning judgments since its survival depends on believing in the reality of guilt rather than forgiveness.

The ego would have us practice "pseudo-forgiveness." In effect, it says, "I can forgive you because I am superior to you. Therefore, I will sit on my anger and repress it, rather than be consciously aware of my desire to kill you, which is what you really deserve." This "pseudo-forgiveness" only reinforces guilt because it is a double message that continues to emphasize the unhealed separation between the "innocent" and the "guilty."

In contrast, the healing and freedom that true forgiveness brings is clearly expressed in this excerpt from a letter I received recently:

> When I truly accept and forgive something I'm released from it and able to let it go. And then, what I truly am and the only thing I've really been withholding is able to flow in, and that's love. And that love is the experience of completeness, at oneness, wholeness. It heals the separateness, the feeling of lack and loss, the feeling of pain, and makes me new and whole, at one.
>
> I think where I go wrong so often is that I become convinced that one of my thoughts, feelings or experiences is THE TRUTH and I get stuck on

either running after it or running away from it. That splitting off in my mind separates me (in my mind at least) from the oneness and puts me in a mistaken state of dis-ease. I need to remember that the goal is one. I have to be willing to accept it all, forgive or give love for it all, say yes to it all in order to experience that perfect wholeness that I am.

A Dream of Forgiveness

Dreams can be very useful in telling us what is happening inside ourselves about guilt. A few years ago I had the following dream, which was very helpful in allowing me to let go of some of my own guilty feelings.

In the dream I was a giant dressed in a football uniform caked with mud from having played on a rain-soaked field. I then found myself in a huge, dark shower stall. As I showered, the mud began to dissolve, and I became smaller and smaller. The smaller my body became, the more the light came into the room. I finally dissolved into nothingness, and the whole room was filled with the most beautiful white light I had ever seen. Since I had been working very hard at forgiving myself and letting go of guilt, my association to the dream was that the mud represented guilt, the water from the shower represented forgiveness, and the light represented love.

I am finding that the only way I can truly be peaceful and happy is to stay in the present by doing my best to make every thought and breath one of forgiveness. This attempt at vigilance is showing me that forgiveness is the key to seeing the world differently; it is the key to happiness and offers us everything that we need. It is a letting go process that releases the past, corrects our misperceptions, and stops the endless recycling of guilt.

*"Love is the way I walk
in gratitude."*

CHAPTER FIVE

Love's Belief System

On the surface level of my ego I still hear the chatter of doubts and uncertainties in my ears, but in the depth of my heart I know that God's love is the answer to all problems. When I permit myself to experience God's love—and give His unconditional love away—I am sane and at peace. When I experience fear, I am insane, riddled with doubts, uncertainties, and worries; and I feel unloved and unloving.

After seeking and searching in many different directions and places, it is exhilarating finally to know what my goal is and how to reach it. I stumble every day; sometimes I fall down; and sometimes it looks as though I am going backwards, but I know that I can no longer retreat. Although my spiritual practice is far from consistent, I know that God is directing my life, and that the peace of God is my goal.

When I give in to the temptation to make condemning

judgments, my peace of mind disappears. When I am able to resist the temptation to judge others, I can see them as teachers of forgiveness in my life, reminding me that I can have peace of mind only when I forgive rather than judge.

Love shows the way to trust and faith that God's love will dissolve all of our difficulties and misunderstandings. To live in love is to be an eternal optimist (and my favorite definition of optimists is those who do not see the clouds because they are walking on them). It is to believe that there are no accidents, no coincidences, and everything that happens to us is according to God's plan and provides a lesson that He would have us learn. A friend of mine recently clarified for me the distinction between a miracle and a coincidence. He said, "a coincidence is a miracle in which God wishes to remain anonymous."

Living in love is living in the freedom of simplicity. It is making our lives a demonstration of the strength of our defenselessness. True humility and meekness can be experienced only when God is our director.

In 1982, my son, Lee, and I had the privilege of traveling and spending some extended time with Mother Teresa in India, as she gave talks in several villages. Lee asked her what she considered the most important traits one must possess in order to serve and help others. She quickly responded, "Humility and meekness."

Mother Teresa also related a story of love and gratitude involving an Indian woman and her eight children who were starving to death. When informed of their plight, Mother Teresa visited the family and brought them a bowl of food. After thanking her, the mother divided the food in half and then suddenly left the house. Upon her return, she shared the remaining half with her eight children. Mother Teresa was perplexed and asked what she had done with the other half of the food. The woman replied, "There is another woman who lives next door; she also has eight starving children. It was only in sharing the food you gave us that my own family could feel blessed with the gift of God's love."

Let us think for a moment what it would be like if we could constantly have total trust and faith in God's love. I think the answer defies our wildest imagination. But somehow I think it would be a state of mind in which we would never worry or feel depressed, angry, fearful, or guilty. Instead we would experience peace, love, and joy all of the time.

It is amazing to me how many people there are who do not remember having even one instant of peace and joy in their lives, but all of us can imagine having that experience for just one second. When we choose to accept the thought system of love and apply it in our lives, we are asked only to do this for one moment, the present instant of now. Giving total and complete love for one second allows us to feel a wholeness and oneness with no sense of separation from others. In that moment of limitless loving and giving, we lose the awareness of our body-self. In remembering God and feeling the presence of His love, this one second becomes a holy instant—a brief glimpse into eternity.

Our challenge is to put these instants together until there is no awareness of time, just love. Although I have experienced a few of these timeless moments, more often than not I have to struggle to put two of these instants together. In all of our relationships, everyone we meet gives us an opportunity to experience a holy instant—one moment when we can join together with no sense of separation, blaming, or judging, knowing God is and feeling His loving presence.

Unconditional Love

In Chapter 3 we defined unconditional love as total acceptance of ourself or another person without qualifications, reservations, or limits of any kind. Unconditional love can only be experienced when we are giving it away and feeling joined in oneness with others. The following statements attempt to summarize what unconditional love is all about:

It is giving our love totally to everyone, excluding no one.

It is loving and giving without expectations, or wanting to get love or anything else in return.

It is total acceptance of another person with no desire to change that person in any way.

It is seeing only the light of love in everyone.

It is having only the desire to accept and experience God's love and to express our gratitude by giving His love away.

A few years ago when I was lecturing in New Zealand, I had an unusual opportunity to attend a Maori tribal funeral. While there, I learned that the Maori Indian tribe had but one word for love—*aroha*—and the literal meaning of that word is unconditional love. I found these people to be most loving, and their love was not conditional or limited to their families. If anyone needed help, regardless of who it might be, it was given. It was a wonderful experience for me to see no false barriers of separation that provide excuses for withholding love. Love was bountiful and joining seemed endless. It occurred to me that all of us have much to learn from these people, who were truly living what many of us regard as an unobtainable ideal.

When we practice unconditional love, we recognize that giving is receiving, and there is no measurement, evaluation, or judgment placed on our love. Jealousy, possessiveness, and competitiveness—which are basic characteristics of the ego's "giving to get" form of love—are totally absent when we offer unconditional love.

The following letter describes a woman who, if she had adhered to the ego's thought system, could very well have ended up chronically angry, depressed, and unhappy. Although still struggling, she chose to forgive, not to blame herself or others, and to live a life of giving love to others. Kathleen is a beautiful witness of what forgiveness and unconditional love are all about.

Dear Dr. Jampolsky,

On Friday I was diagnosed as having active TB. On Saturday my husband left permanently after nine years of marriage and nine months of continuous storm; and that Sunday my father died. Looking back now I think all that I would need to say to make this tale a "soap opera" would be that on Monday one of my children died. But, gratefully, not so!

I returned to nursing (after my Petri dishes stopped growing A and B cells!), and it was cancer patients and their families who helped heal me. One day I recognized in their faces and in the depths of their eyes all the pain and grief so freshly etched on my soul. But most of all, I remembered what comfort felt like from the few who had courage enough to extend it to me when I was a gaping wound. I understood death and dying, for a part of me was gone forever. But what those patients gave me was life as I have begun to know it—they allowed me to love them into eternity and, by doing so, gave me the vision of my unique dignity.

Although over these past seven years I have repaired some of the injuries (I have openly forgiven my ex-husband and his wife, and we share our three children without constraint), I have continued to grow in new relationships.

Today I am a director of nursing at a nearby nursing home, and on my office door "Teach Only Love" is all that is written. Traffic flows constantly, but there is an unwritten agreement that once inside, you can discuss anything as long as it is not demeaning to others *or* to yourself.

Thank you, Dr. Jampolsky, for your encouragement. But even more than that, for inviting me to be all that I am without fear.

(signed) *Kathleen*

In attempting to experience more unconditional love in our lives, it can be helpful to review the following statements.

How Is Unconditional Love Accomplished?

By letting go of all our guilt and not projecting guilt onto others.

By forgiving and letting go of the past, staying in the present and living in the joy of now.

By not making demands on anyone.

By resisting the temptation to judge.

By giving all of our needs, wants, desires, and feelings of scarcity to our inner teacher, and letting the voice of love transform them into fullness and wholeness.

By making each moment an opportunity for offering forgiveness to someone in our lives; and for seeing everyone as our teacher—thus giving ourselves the opportunity to practice and learn the benefits of forgiveness.

By feeling the love of God within us and reminding ourselves of our thankfulness to Him for the completeness of His eternal love.

By recognizing that when we know our identity is love, we have no need except to extend that love endlessly.

The Spirit of Love/God

Our intellect, with all its analyzing, is not able to experience God. Only our hearts can do that. Just as the immediate appreciation of a beautiful sunset would be destroyed for us if we were asked to analyze and compare it with other sunsets we have seen, so must we go beyond intellectualizing and analyzing if we are to experience God. God, being love, is beyond what words can define and can only be felt when we are willing to let go of our need for categorizing and evaluating our experience. Feeling God's presence is always related to giving love and being joined or at one with another person.

Having been an atheist for most of my life, "God" used to be a negative, knee-jerk word for me, a turnoff; and whenever the word "God" was mentioned in conversation, I would either stop listening or leave. I now know that there are many people like myself who have felt—or feel— that either God or their religion has let them down, so the whole area of spirituality has remained a sensitive one for them.

To those who continue to feel vulnerable in this area, it can be most helpful to forgive whatever lingering misperceptions we have regarding our past spiritual beliefs. Then it is possible to see God simply as a nonphysical love force that is neither vengeful, judgmental, nor punishing—only loving and forgiving. Being able to experience God as a loving force, and a light shining within me and throughout the universe at all times, is very different from my childhood concept of God as an old man with a beard, way up in the sky, distant and external, waiting to judge me.

One does not have to be religious or on a spiritual pathway to acknowledge and agree that it is our attachment to fear and guilt that prevents us from knowing that our only true reality is love. Our relationships will be healed only when we are willing to let go of fear and guilt by forgiving others and ourselves. As we become more consistent in applying the principles of love in our lives, we naturally develop an awareness of a power greater than ourselves. Whether we call this power "the source," "the force," "the creator," or "God," it is the spirit of love.

In love's belief system, our identity, our reality, and the truth are all the same as they blend into the oneness of love. Our ego, however, would tell us that there are many different kinds of love. Love's belief system teaches us there is only one love—God's love—and that it is a living force shining within each of us. It is beyond measurement and undefinable; it can be experienced only on an equal basis, and its only properties are extension and expansion.

When I am tempted to confuse what is real with what is not, I have found this simple rule of thumb helpful. If something is real, it fits the definition of being eternal and is therefore true. Truth is constantly extending and expanding, yet changeless and everlasting. The only example I know that fits this definition is God's love, which is our true identity and the essence of our being.

As adults, we frequently hold on to fearful events that occurred in our childhood, which causes us to mistrust God or to forget about Him. Last year I was able to let go of one of those childhood fears.

I had given a seminar with Carol Howe on "A Course in Miracles" for Windstar, John Denver's foundation in Aspen, Colorado, and after the presentation, John invited me to have lunch with him. While we were eating, he asked me if I had ever flown in a private plane before. I replied, "Yes, many times. My son, Lee, used to fly." He then asked me if I would like to go for a ride in his airplane, and I immediately said yes. Although it was cold, snowing slightly, and the ceiling was low, John said it was perfectly safe for flying.

When we got to the airport, before I knew what was happening, he was strapping me into one of those "Snoopy" World War I airplane fighter pilot masks and fastening a parachute onto my back. Then, out of the hangar came a biplane with open cockpits. I had thought we would be flying in a plane like a Cessna where I would be sitting safely inside a closed cabin!

My heart began to pound wildly with fear. I thought to myself, biplanes are used for stunt flying—all my childhood fears began rushing in upon me. As a kid I was terrified of roller coasters, and my stomach always got queasy with any change of motion.

Those thoughts were enough for me. I started to tell John that no way was I going to go up in that plane. Then all of a sudden that little inner voice—the voice of love, like inner dictation—said, "Just be still. When you know God's love, there is nothing to fear." So I changed my mind and signaled John a weak "okay."

He put me in the front cockpit, which was equipped with earphones and a microphone so I could talk with him, and we took off. Then the most amazing thing happened! We flew all around for about thirty minutes, and it was fun. I had absolutely no fear.

And then panic struck. John said into his microphone, "Hey, Jerry, how would you like me to do a stunt?" I began impulsively to say the words, "NO WAY!" when, once again, I was interrupted by that silent voice with the same message. I gave John another—although this time much more feeble—"okay."

He described exactly what he was going to do—a 360-degree loop. John did precisely what he said he was going to do, and guess what? To my surprise, I did not vomit the black bean soup I had for lunch. Instead, I enjoyed every second of our adventure, and I was absolutely astonished to hear myself request, "John, can we do it again?" And we did.

I was ever so grateful to John for offering me an opportunity to let go of my fearful past and not let it be superimposed on the present. I was happy that at least in that instant I listened to my inner voice, the voice of love, instead of the voice of fear. What a joy it was to experience that God is always present! What a joy it was to live only in the now and to learn that I can't love myself or others unconditionally until I let go of all the fear I have been hanging on to.

When we are at one with God, we are not aware of any sense of bodily limitation. Nor are we aware of forms of any kind that continue to change. We do not equate life with a body moving in time and space. We do not see death as real, but rather experience life and love as extending forever.

My rational mind still has its daily fights with God, but at the same time, there seem to be more and more moments of divine awakening when I experience peace, certainty, and serenity, knowing that God loves me now and always. And when I remember God, depression, pain, and frustration simply disappear because I am reminded that I have everything that I need, and that I lack nothing. For the first time in my life, "God is love" is no longer a silly, inane statement to me, but something I am actually experiencing now.

Choosing between the Two Thought Systems

Every decision we make in our lives is chosen either from the ego's thought system or love's thought system.

The ego would have us base all of our decisions on the condemning judgments we have made in the past. Love's thought system would have us release the past and make all of our decisions by listening to the voice of our inner teacher, the voice of love.

The following chart can be used to help us clarify which of these thought systems we are choosing to live by:

Ego's Thought System

1. This moment is for guilt and fear; the fearful past predicts the fearful, guilty present and future. Spend most of your time worrying about the past and future, and don't experience much joy now.

2. Our reality is limited to our body, and it is impossible to live in this world without fear, depression, conflict, and worry.

3. When we try to get as much as we can and hold on to it, we are experiencing ourselves as fearful and separate from others.

4. Age and experience determine who our teachers are.

5. Love is always conditional; I will love you *if* you perform and behave as I want you to.

6. There are different kinds and degrees of love: a love for this, a love for that. And there are people who should be excluded from love because of their unworthy behavior.

7. The body, life, and love all die. Life and the body are the same. Life and love are separate.

8. Love is limited to what we see and hear. It has boundaries and expectations.

9. Everything we see is separate and different from what we are.

10. What is true is that we are born to live in the world where sooner or later we will experience frustration, pain, unhappiness, despair, fear, hopelessness, and death. There are a lot of things besides love in this world.

Love's Thought System

1. This moment is the only moment there is, and it is for love. In this moment there is no guilt or fear.

2. Our natural state of being is love. It is to be happy, joyful, and peaceful.

3. When we constantly give our love and peace away and join in oneness with others, we are experiencing ourselves as love.

4. Everyone, regardless of age, is our teacher of love.

5. Love is always unconditional and has nothing to do with performance or behavior.

6. There is only love. It is always changeless, maximal, and nonexclusive.

7. Life is separate from the body; life and love are one and the same; and life is always—because love never dies.

8. Love has no limits, boundaries, or expectations. It simply unfolds upon itself.

9. Everything we see is but a mirror of what we are.

10. Love is the only thing that can be true, and what is love is all there is.

*"Let every voice but God's be
still in me."*

CHAPTER SIX

Love Is Listening

Listening

A few years ago I was lecturing in New Zealand and had an opportunity to visit a hospice unit in a general hospital for people who were critically ill and facing death. I was introduced to one of the volunteers. On her lapel was her name, and underneath it was one word that told me everything about her. That one word was "Listener." It told me and everyone else who met her that her job wasn't to give advice or to offer so-called constructive criticism; she was there to give unconditional love and offer total acceptance by listening. Listening is love and love is listening.

We often interrupt other people before they have finished speaking. And frequently we tune them out long before we interrupt, because we are busy preparing our response. What *we* have to say becomes more important than what the other person is trying to tell us. Listening with undivided attention and unconditional love is perhaps the greatest gift we can extend to others.

The Voice of Love (Voice of God, Holy Spirit)

To give the gift of listening to others, we first must learn to listen to the voice of love within ourselves. For most of us it seems difficult to remember, as was mentioned in the preceding chapter, that as long as we live in the world, we have to make decisions based on one of two voices: the voice of the ego, or the voice of love.

The voice of love goes by many names, such as the voice of God, Holy Spirit, voice of knowing, inner teacher, inner voice, inner guide, and intuition. The voice of God has nothing to do with our past experiences, our intellectual or rational mind, or our common sense. It comes from the core of the knowledge of love, the God-self, that is in the center of our being—always there to answer and give us directions in response to any questions that we may ask.

Stilling the Mind

In order to hear this inner guidance, we need to learn to still our minds, have the faith and a little willingness to ask for help—and expect to have our request answered. The voice, or guidance, can come to us as a thought; it can be experienced as inner dictation, or it can be a visualized form such as a traffic light signaling green for us to go, red to stop, or yellow to be cautious.

Our minds are very undisciplined. Thousands of uncontrolled thoughts, continually recycling our past, race through our minds each minute. One of the most powerful barriers to stilling our mind is the static created by the ego's attraction to guilt and thoughts of fear. It is very difficult to experience peace while we are being bombarded by these endless thoughts and distracting external stimuli.

In order to perceive the world differently, it is imperative that we learn to retrain our minds and realize that we can gain control over our thoughts, that we can choose the thoughts we want to have in our minds. A disciplined mind is a free mind, and our goal *is* freedom. If we continue to be dominated by our egos, we will be unable to free ourselves from the bondage of fear, guilt, and limitations. Retraining the mind takes work. To retrain our minds, we must learn the value of stilling the mind—the value of quiet time.

There are many ways of stilling the mind, such as meditation, prayer, the use of mental imagery through active imagination, etc. Rather than go into detail about these processes, I would like to share a simplified way of looking at them.

Meditation can be viewed as a focused concentration, which may or may not be on God, that allows for self-exploration and increased self-awareness that occur when the mind becomes still. Some people experience meditation as a doorway to prayer.

Prayer can be thought of as focused concentration or communication with God. On the lowest level, prayer is asking, and on the highest level it is listening, loving, and expressing gratitude to God. Meister Eckhart, the German mystic, describes prayer very succinctly when he states, "If the only prayer you say in your whole life is 'thank you,' that would suffice."

In both prayer and meditation, there is a decision to go inward and not to be affected by the noise of the external world. At a given point, meditation and prayer may become one. There is an old saying that a busy mind is a sick mind, a slow mind is a healthy mind, and a still mind is a divine mind.

Let us not be concerned about technical distinctions between meditation or prayer, but let us make the stilling of our minds in the morning on awakening and in the evening before going to sleep a top priority.

My own way of detaching myself from the chaotic thoughts that race through my mind is to remind myself, once again, that the peace of God is my only goal. For just one second I concentrate on emptying myself of worldly needs and desires. In that instant I open my heart to God's love, asking to be His messenger and to see His will and mine as one. In the quiet that frequently follows, I may experience myself as God's light lighting up the world, lighting up all minds as one. For that one second I feel the peace and happiness of God's boundless love, which is often accompanied by a feeling that I need do nothing but be.

If quieting the mind is something new for you, begin by committing yourself to still the mind for no longer than three minutes in the morning and three minutes in the evening, gradually increasing this time according to your own inner guidance. It is important to be patient and gentle with yourself, and to resist the temptation to categorize, evaluate, or judge how well you are doing.

At the end of this chapter you will find some suggestions for stilling the mind, including the use of active imagination. Active imagination is a way in which we can use mental imagery to focus on just one thing, such as seeing ourselves peacefully sitting by a beautiful, quiet lake in order to still the many thoughts in our minds.

Learning to Listen

Listening to our inner voice, the voice of love, means laying aside our rational, analytical, deductive mind and being led by the love center in our heart. Our ego does not want to make this easy for us and tries to persuade us that making decisions on such an irrational basis is foolish and insane.

In 1979, I had a powerful experience as a result of trying to listen to my inner voice. I was scheduled to lecture in Israel on May 1 and was looking forward to spending a few days sightseeing and exploring the historical landmarks after my talk. About two weeks before leaving for the Middle East, my inner voice instructed me to change my tickets and go to Egypt on May 3.

Since I had no Egyptian friends, the whole idea of making such a trip seemed ridiculous and insane. However, my guidance was insistent, so I finally exchanged my tickets for a flight to Cairo. I was careful not to mention this to anyone because I thought they would think I was crazy, but I did tell my good friend and co-author, Bill Thetford. I ended my conversation with Bill with a rather flip remark: "I don't know what I am supposed to do there—maybe I am supposed to see someone famous whom I admire, like Mrs. Jihan Sadat."

In those days, you could not fly directly from Israel to Egypt, but had to stop in Greece first. En route from Athens to Cairo as I was reading the airline magazine, I came across a story about Dr. Shahbender, head of the Egyptian Cancer Institute. It occurred to me that since I didn't know why I was making this trip, perhaps it was to meet Dr. Shahbender.

The next morning, after much difficulty, I was finally able to reach him by phone. He replied, "I'm sorry, but since today is Friday I cannot see you. It is like Sunday in the United States, and I am going to the country with my family." Then there was a brief pause, and he said, "Well, if you could come in a taxi right away, I could see you for about ten minutes."

When I met him at his residence, there was an instant rapport between us, as if we had known each other for centuries. Almost immediately he invited me to join him and his family for a visit to the country. To my surprise, when we reached our destination, it turned out to be an informal party that included most of Mr. Sadat's cabinet. I met the minister of health, who invited me to his office the next day.

During our visit the next day, he said he wanted Mrs. Sadat to meet me and promptly made arrangements for me to go to her residence in Giza. When he told me that, goose flesh appeared all over my body as I remembered that flip remark I had made to Bill before I left.

When I did meet Mrs. Sadat, the five-minute talk I was scheduled for turned into an hour-long interview. Since our initial meeting, Mrs. Sadat and I have communicated regularly, and in recent years we have lectured together on the topic of "Children as Teachers of Peace" in both the United States and Europe.

When I returned to California and reflected on all that had happened, I realized that it was not just the experiences I had had in Egypt that were so powerful, but it was the recognition that none of this could have occurred without my inner listening. As a result, I have been more willing to trust my inner voice and follow its guidance—even when it seems irrational.

Fear of Death

How death is looked upon is one of the most important differences between the two belief systems. The greatest threat our ego-self holds over us is the fear of death that causes interference with listening. As long as we identify with our body, fear and guilt will be lodged somewhere in our mind—even though it may be disguised and not in our conscious awareness. Guilt always results, in some way, in an attack either on ourselves or on others. It is guilt that reinforces the ego's belief in the past, present, and future—a time sequence in which the death of the body is equated with the end of life. Our ego keeps us preoccupied with efforts to control others and the world around us in an attempt to deny our fear of death.

In love's belief system, death is considered to be the transition from form to formlessness. In the state of formlessness, life and love are the same and continue forever; they do not come to an end when the costume we call the body is laid aside.

When we are free of guilt, we are living each instant as though it were timeless, with the knowledge that we are love, we are life, and we are eternal because God is eternal. When we are free of guilt, there is no fear of death.

Not long ago I received a beautiful letter from a woman named Lory. Her brother, Ray, was killed in an automobile accident at the age of twenty-seven. She enclosed a letter he had written five years earlier giving instructions about how he would like to be remembered after his death.

I believe you will agree with me that Ray understood with great clarity that to give is to live, and that life and love are forever and do not end with physical death.

Dear Dr. Jampolsky,

There are no words to tell you how very grateful I am to you for taking the time to call my mother on December 26. In Spanish, we have a saying and, loosely translated, it says, "May God return it all to you," and I hope and pray that all the love you have shown us is returned to you, a thousand times over.

I must tell you how much I enjoyed *Teach Only Love*. I used some of your words not only for personal comfort, but in the eulogy I wrote for my brother Ray. Ray had a marvelous gift of living every moment. He also found and made the time to listen, to anyone, anytime. One of God's greatest gifts to me was the twenty-seven years I had with Ray. Now my parents struggle with the reality of having to bury a child.

After Ray's funeral, we found the paper I am enclosing. Ray wrote this five years ago when he was only twenty-two. To me, it was so eloquent in its heartfelt simplicity that I thought you might like a copy.

God bless you.

Love and light to you,
Lory

Ray's "Bed of Life" Instructions

TO REMEMBER ME!

The day will come when my body will lie upon a white sheet neatly tucked under four corners of a mattress located in a hospital busily occupied with the living and the dying. At a certain moment a doctor will determine that my brain has ceased to function and that, for all intents and purposes, my life has stopped.

When this happens, do not attempt to instill artificial life into my body by the use of a machine. And don't call this my deathbed. Let it be called the Bed of Life, and let my body be taken from it to help others live fuller lives.

Give my sight to the man who has never seen a sunrise, a baby's face, or love in the eyes of a woman. Give my heart to a person whose own heart has caused nothing but endless days of pain. Give my blood to the teenager who was pulled from the wreckage of his car, so that he might live to see his grandchildren play. Give my kidneys to one who depends on a machine to exist from week to week. Take my bones, every muscle, every fiber and nerve in my body and find a way to make a crippled child walk.

Explore every corner of my brain, take my cells,

if necessary, and let them grow so that, someday, a speechless boy will shout at the crack of a bat and a deaf girl will hear the sound of rain against her window.

Burn what is left of me and scatter the ashes to the winds to help the flowers grow.

If you must bury something, let it be my faults, my weaknesses, and all prejudice against my fellow man.

Give my sins to the devil, my soul to God.

If, by chance, you wish to remember me, do it with a kind deed or word to someone who needs you. If you do all I have asked, I will live forever.

This is my wish.

Ray

Resistance to Hearing the Inner Voice

Our ego likes to increase our doubt by constantly raising questions such as, "Are you really sure that the voice you are hearing is the voice of love? Maybe you're simply fooling yourself." Our ego voice wants to be heard first. It tries to convince us not to risk turning over our will to God because we may not like the answer. For sure, my ego still taunts me with these games, leaving me in conflict and uncertainty. Yet, the more I am willing to trust the voice of love, the more peace and confidence I experience.

I frequently get caught in the rationalization that I will be only too happy to do God's will if He agrees to go along with mine. What that means is that if I have already determined the answer I want, I will truly be unable to ask a real question. Coming to God with empty hands means not being invested with a specific answer. That is what causes my ego to go wild because its survival depends on getting answers that will give it its own way. It is only when I am attached to the outcome that my ego raises the static, which interferes with hearing the inner voice.

It is not necessary for us to have let go of our anger, guilt, and unforgiving thoughts before we come to our inner teacher. It is our willingness, however partial, to turn our problems over to our inner guide that makes it possible for our misperceptions to be transformed. As we are increasingly willing to listen only to the voice of love, we can begin to recognize that our assignment here on earth is to be a messenger of God, who offers unconditional love to everyone. However, before we can be messengers of God, we must first receive and accept the message for ourselves.

Light of Love, Light of Christ

Ten years ago, if I were reading a book that mentioned such things as the light of the world, the light of love, the Christ light, I would have put it down in disgust and not opened it again. So I had some initial reluctance about using these terms in this book, with the thought that many of you might have a similar reaction. Yet, to learn to know that we are the light of the world, and that the light is blocked from our awareness by guilt and fear, is an essential part of this book.

The light of love, the Christ light, can be looked upon as light radiating from the center of the heart of God. It radiates to and through us to all others. For our purpose here, the light of love, the Christ light, the light of God, and the light of the world are all terms that can be used interchangeably. We can also look upon the light as the creative source of energy for the universe. Each of us is here on the planet earth to act as substations for emitting that light, so that all the darkness of guilt, fear, and separation can disappear. We heal our minds when we join with each other as one by seeing only the light of love in others and ourselves. In our healing, we recognize that there are no separate minds, that minds are joined and that there is only one universal mind joined with the heart of God.

I find the following analogy helpful in understanding the universal mind. I close my eyes and imagine the whole universe to be made up of water. I then drop a pebble of love into the water, seeing a ripple go out which affects every particle of the water. And then the ripple comes back to affect me. In a similar manner, when we send the light of love in our heart to all others, it affects their minds and then returns to us. It removes all doubt about ourselves and who we are.

There is a very powerful passage about the light of Christ from *A Course in Miracles*. When I am feeling doubtful and uncertain about life and myself, reading this has been enormously helpful in lifting my spirits and making it possible for me to hear the voice of love again. If you find that you are uncomfortable with or have a negative attachment to the word "Christ," simply substitute the word "love" for "Christ." Following is the quotation* from the course arranged in poetic form:

The sight of Christ is all there is to see.
The song of Christ is all there is to hear.
The hand of Christ is all there is to hold.
There is no journey but to walk with Him.

* * * *

There must be doubt before there can be conflict.
And every doubt must be about yourself.
Christ has no doubt, and from His certainty
His quiet comes.

He will exchange His certainty for all your doubts,
If you agree that He is one with you,
And that this oneness is endless, timeless,
And within your grasp because your hands are His.

*A Course in Miracles, Text, p. 475.

He is within you, yet He walks beside you and before,
Leading the way that He must go to find Himself
Complete. His quietness becomes your certainty.
And where is doubt when certainty has come?

Breaking the Resistance

There are many different spiritual pathways, each with a teacher—living or dead—who serves as a model for learning. It may not be essential to have a master teacher to identify with, but for many of us it can be helpful.

I used to look at God and my inner teacher in an abstract way, and I found it very difficult indeed to feel a close, personal relationship with these abstractions. Yet I also have been resistant to gurus, master teachers, or identification with a personalized inner teacher—particularly if his name was Jesus.

Nevertheless, I felt I needed to let go of my old ideas about Jesus and try to become more open-minded about who he was and what he represented. I was not prepared for what happened next, however. To my complete surprise, I began to develop what I would call a personal relationship with Jesus. First, I began to see Jesus as a messenger of God who came to teach the world forgiveness and love. Then I began to view him as an older brother and a master teacher who demonstrated that it was possible to let go completely of judgments, guilt, and everything that is valued in this world except God's love. More important, for me, he demonstrated that death was not real, that life is eternal, and that minds can communicate with each other forever, even after the body has been laid aside.

I began to feel his presence in me, and at times I actually felt he was acting through me as an extension of his thoughts, his words, and his actions. I became absorbed by his message that the world could be transformed if all of us would practice forgiveness. At first, I was concerned about what other people might think of me, so I kept my relationship with Jesus a secret.

Then one day as I was meditating at Johns Hopkins Medical School before giving a lecture there, I asked if it was all right to use the word "God" or "Christ" in my talk. The inner answer I received was a definite "no."

After the lecture, which was very well received, a professor of psychiatry escorted me out of the building through a different door from the one by which I had entered. I was deeply involved in conversation with him, not looking where I was going, when suddenly I bumped into a large structure. I looked up, and, to my amazement, I saw the largest, most peaceful and joyful statue of Jesus I had ever seen. I found myself shouting, "What is Jesus doing here in Johns Hopkins University?"

The professor laughed and said that the door through which I had initially entered the hospital was the new entrance, called the cancer entrance. The door I was leaving by was the original entrance, called the Christ entrance. The statue had been at Johns Hopkins since the school was built. That experience symbolized for me that the Christ light, the Christ spirit, the light of love is always with me, and I do not necessarily have to call it by name.

I was so impressed with that statue that I asked for a photograph of it, which is now on the wall of my bedroom. However, I still was not ready to have a picture of Jesus in my living room for everyone to see. As my relationship with Jesus has become more comfortable, I am now less concerned about what others might say, and today a prominent picture of Jesus hangs in my living room over the fireplace.

At this point, I need to say parenthetically, and as clearly as I know how, that to heal relationships, we do not have to have a relationship with Jesus or to see him, or anyone else, as a master teacher. I only want to share with you that in a way which I cannot fully explain, I have chosen Jesus as my teacher and have found that helpful. But I am surely not suggesting that others must do the same.

Faith and Trust

In the thought system of love, faith can be thought of as trusting in God and having the inner certainty of knowing without any doubt that we are always safe, and that we will never be left comfortless. It is trusting that God loves us completely and eternally, and that the power of His love is always in us. It is knowing unequivocally that we can trust His strength rather than the limited, meager strength of our personality-self, and that there are no problems that God's love cannot solve.

A Child's Trust in God's Love

Recently at our center, I participated in an intake interview with a ten-year-old boy, named Derek Schmidt, who had leukemia. Prior to our meeting it had looked as though his cancerous condition had disappeared; but suddenly it had reappeared, and his family brought him to us for help. For the first time since the onset of his illness, his parents had lost faith and trust in God, feeling "how can we trust God when our prayers went unanswered?"

Tears of gratitude came to my eyes as their son said, "You don't have to understand everything to have faith and trust in God; all you have to know is that God loves us all the time, and that nothing ever happens to us that we cannot handle with His help."

To me, he was a wise soul in a young body, reminding all of us what faith and trust are all about. The day I saw this boy, I badly needed this loving reminder since I was having my own problems with faith and trust. His simplicity, innocence, and clarity were a great help to me in restoring my own faith and trust.

Suggestions for Stilling the Mind

Following are five practical exercises for learning to still the mind and activate the concept of love through listening. Repeat each of these exercises initially for three to five minutes, continuing for longer periods of time if you find it comfortable to do so.

1. I AM RELAXED

   Close your eyes, go inside yourself, and find a quiet place where you feel peaceful.

   As you breathe in, say the words, "I am," silently to yourself.

   As you breathe out, say the word, ". . . relaxed," silently to yourself.

   Keep as your single focus, "I am relaxed."

2. INHALE LOVE; EXHALE PEACE AND JOY

   Play some music that you find relaxing.

   As you inhale, experience yourself breathing in unconditional love.

As you exhale, experience yourself breathing out peace and joy to all the world and every living thing in it.

3. BECOMING ONE WITH LIGHT

Light a candle and concentrate only on the radiance of the light.

Feel the reflection of the light in every aspect of your being.

Experience yourself becoming one with the light.

Say to yourself silently, "I am the light of the world."

Experience both friends and enemies walking into the light, becoming one with the light and you.

4. BECOMING ONE WITH A FLOWER

Use your imagination and visualize your favorite flower.

Imagine that you can detach yourself from your body for a few minutes; then go inside the flower and imagine yourself becoming one with every part of it.

Feel yourself receiving unconditional love from the rays of the sun.

Experience the essence of your being, your love and beauty, radiating in every direction for all to behold.

In this relaxed state experience the giving and receiving of love as one.

5. LET GO,* LET GOD

Close your eyes.

Inhale with the word "Let."

Exhale with the word ". . . go."

Inhale with the word "Let."

Exhale with the word ". . . God."

*LET GO, that is, old attachments to the past, old beliefs.

*"All fear is past and only
love is here."*

CHAPTER SEVEN

A Bridge to Heaven on Earth

The material in this chapter can be used as a bridge that leads us from the belief in our egos to the belief in love. I have included some exercises and charts to be used as guides for closing the gap between our allegiance to the world of the ego and the recognition of our reality in the world of love.

Heaven on Earth

Heaven can be thought of not as a place, but a state of mind. It is the experience of oneness with each other and God, of limitless peace, joy, and love. For most of us, to experience that state of mind for just one second requires a shift in perception that at first may seem difficult to make. On the other hand, "difficult" is a word that is based on our past beliefs that there are limits to our learning ability.

We do not have to relive the past and its difficulties. We do not have to procrastinate. We can choose right now to have that one second of heaven on earth.

When our mind remains still and completely at peace, unlimited joy can be experienced—a joy beyond all imagination. Following is a chart of the attributes of our mind when it is experiencing heaven on earth.

HEAVEN ON EARTH

PEACE	PATIENCE
LOVE	GENTLENESS
SERENITY	LIGHT-HEARTEDNESS
KINDNESS	LAUGHTER
TENDERNESS	HAPPINESS

As I have mentioned earlier, when we know with certainty that our natural state is love, we also know that nothing can threaten us. These attributes then radiate from us spontaneously without our having to think about them and with nothing to block their expression.

On the other hand, when we are not certain and have doubts about who and what we are, guilt and fear will block the expression of these positive, happy emotions.

Forgiveness

True forgiveness is the bridge we walk across that releases us from guilt and fear, and allows us to experience heaven on earth.

In the following chart, which is a prescription for inner peace, please note that the first four steps are about forgiveness. Practicing forgiveness is the key to freedom from guilt in our lives. By consistently applying the ten tenets in this prescription, we can transform our lives and the world we see.

PRESCRIPTION FOR INNER PEACE

1. Forgive our parents totally.

2. Forgive everyone who has ever been here, who is here now, or who will be here in the future, including ourselves, totally.

3. Forgive the world totally.

4. Forgive God totally.

5. Take a leap in faith and trust in love, trust God.

6. Choose to experience peace rather than conflict.

7. Choose to experience love rather than fear and guilt.

8. Choose to be a love-finder rather than a fault-finder.

9. Choose to be a love-giver rather than a love-seeker.

10. Teach only love.

The purpose of forgiveness is to help us see there is no value in guilt. For forgiveness to be completely effective, it must be total. Ninety-five percent forgiveness doesn't work. It is like the frequent analogy made about pregnancy—either you are pregnant or you are not.

We can never hurt or be hurt unless we believe that our reality is identified with our body rather than our spirit. When we identify only with the true reality of our light and the light of others, the process of forgiveness then permits us to let go of whatever we think people have done to us, or whatever we think we did to them. It is like dreaming that someone has hurt us and waking up still feeling that our dream was real. Only when we remember it was nothing but a dream are we able to dismiss the whole incident as unreal. Similarly, forgiveness helps us let go of our illusory past so we can experience love in the present as our only reality. Forgiveness allows us to see that what we thought was a sin calling for guilt and punishment is only a mistake that needs correction, not punishment.

Forgiveness is Letting Go

Children are wonderful teachers of forgiveness. Several years ago I was a consultant for a large transportation company. On one of my visits to this company, I took along a twelve-year-old boy named Tony who had cancer, and who was an active member of the children's group at the center. At the meeting, one of the regional managers expressed a great deal of anger because a competing company had lured away one of his key employees, and he felt it would be difficult to replace him. I asked Tony what he might say that could be helpful.

Tony asked the man if he felt upset, and the manager said, "Yes." Then Tony said, "If you could be any place in the world that you wanted to be, where you could be relaxed and feel peaceful, where would that be?" The answer was, "Hawaii." Tony suggested to the manager that he close his eyes and imagine that he was in Hawaii, feeling relaxed, at one with the warm sand, sky, and water. He went on to say, "You know, mister, you can't be relaxed or feel peaceful as long as you are angry. You won't be able to make wise decisions until you forgive, not just your competitor, but the guy he took away. Forgiveness is letting go—letting the incident flow away."

Later, the manager came up to me and said, "You know, Jerry, if you had told me the same thing, I wouldn't have been receptive, but when a twelve-year-old boy told me these things, they seem so simple and right on."

Most of us live in the world in a state of anguish, wondering who or what will attack us next. How can we get rid of these fearful thoughts? It is not as complicated as we think, providing we are willing to let go of the old belief system. As we have just seen, children have a way of making seemingly complicated things clear and simple. Forgiveness is the answer. It allows the miracle of love to take place so we can heal our relationships and recognize that there is no separation.

We cannot teach love and be consistently loving until we stop blaming others and ourselves. *We cannot demonstrate total love until we have healed all of our relationships.* Forgiveness is the key to happiness because it removes all blocks to fear and guilt, and allows us to live in a world of all-inclusive love.

Check-in Points in Going Home to God

There are times when I have found that nothing seems to help me forgive, and that I have chosen to hang on to fear. Not very long ago I found myself quite depressed, feeling that I had been hurt and rejected by someone very close to me. It felt very real—not illusory—and it didn't seem as though I was responsible for what I saw, but that someone else was actually hurting me. The principles that I have mentioned in this book seemed like idle, hollow rhetoric to me. I was stuck and did not seem to be able—nor did I even want—to change my mind. I certainly didn't feel God's presence or His love, and I even began to doubt His existence in my life. In fact, doubts about almost everything popped up in my mind, and I began to wonder if I really understood what it meant to be on a spiritual pathway.

Later, after I was finally able to quiet myself and ask for help and inner guidance, I wrote the following check-in points in going home to God. Needless to say, I had flunked all ten points, and I began to see how the distortions and deceptions of my ego had tricked me into believing I was separate from God. You may find, as I did, that it is helpful to take one of these check-in points each day and attempt to apply it to all situations.

Check-in Points

1. Am I willing to see any problem—regardless of its form—all guilt, pain, and frustration, as a statement that my ego-mind is fearful of God and is choosing to be separate from God? Am I willing to be responsible for what I see?

2. Am I holding on to guilt and making a judgment against someone else or myself, or am I being forgiving?

3. Do I truly trust that God's will for me is perfect happiness right now?

4. Do I see the purpose of this relationship as always for joining and not for separation?

5. Is my interest in everyone the same as my interest in myself, or am I only concerned about my personal ego needs?

6. Am I interested in getting rather than giving?

7. Am I trying to control or manipulate anyone else in my life?

8. Am I choosing to demand, rather than to love?

9. Do I truly have faith and trust that God loves me completely, perfectly, and eternally?

10. Am I determined to make life *my* plan, or am I willing to accept God's plan for my life?

Mental Imagery in Forgiveness

Many people have told me that the following mental imagery exercise in forgiveness has been of considerable help to them.

Close your eyes. Use your imagination to see yourself in front of a very special microscope. While you are looking into the microscope, imagine you can see your own individual heart cells; look carefully and you will see they are round cells with smiling faces. These faces are smiling because they are completely full and saturated with love. They have everything they need within them; they need nothing from the outside. Their love just extends and expands, asking no questions and making no judgments. Each cell is a microcosm of you and me. Our identity, like the cell's identity, is boundless love, and in our true state, we do not need anything from the outside.

If you look carefully with your imagination, you will be able to see the energy radiating from the love in the cell as a white light getting brighter and brighter. See the white light obliterating the cellular membrane and joining the white light from all the other heart cells. Now see your heart as a beautiful, pulsating white light getting brighter all the time. That light is a reflection of God's love. Say to yourself silently, "I am the light of the world."

Now, use your imagination to its fullest. Visualize that light going to all the other cells in your body. See your body being transformed into a beam of light. Next, see your light joining and merging with all the other beams of light in the universe until there is just one universal light—continuing to get brighter and brighter.

Now think of someone who irritates or depresses you—someone you have not totally forgiven. Let go of the guilty misperception that you have ever hurt this person or that he/she has ever hurt you. Let go of the past and see it as a dream that has vanished. Use your imagination and see that person walking into the light and becoming that light and, as you do that, say to yourself:

I forgive you *and* me—both one and the same.

Now I can say "good-bye to guilt and blame."

The last chart in this chapter is suggestions for making alive the principles of truth. These suggestions can be considered a daily guideline to help us control the thoughts in our mind and apply the lessons in this book each day.

SUGGESTIONS FOR MAKING THE PRINCIPLES OF TRUTH ALIVE

1. As you awaken in the morning, remind yourself right away that peace of mind, peace of God, is the only goal you want today.

2. To have this peace, choose to release any negative thoughts of fear, guilt, and pain that you may have found in your mind on awakening.

   Close your eyes and imagine the rays of the sun as God's love directed as a beam of light toward the center of your heart.

   Next, feel the light of love extend out from your heart, radiating throughout your body.

   Experience the light extending out from you, joining with every living thing in this world, excluding no one.

3. Remind yourself that God's will for you today is perfect happiness. With a smile on your face and in your heart go out into the world and extend your happiness to all whom you meet.

4. Decide today that you will not give the power to make you happy or miserable to people or conditions in your external world.

5. After you have read each day's lesson in the morning, allow at least ten minutes of quiet time for the lesson to become part of yourself.

Throughout the day, once each hour if possible, review the principle and apply it to the day's activities.

In the evening, before bedtime, take ten minutes to go over the lessons once again. Let go of any negative thoughts you have held on to during the day. Then relax and allow yourself to experience the peace of God.

PART II

Introduction

The following fourteen lessons demonstrate ways in which the concepts we have been discussing in Part I can be directly applied in situations you are likely to encounter in your everyday life.

At the end of each lesson you will find several steps for integrating that day's lesson into your daily life experiences. It is not essential for your learning that you complete each of these steps. Some of the suggestions will seem more natural for you to follow than others. What is important is to do your best and, above all, *do not feel guilty* about what you perceive as your progress.

These lessons can help us learn that we are responsible for what we see and experience. And in recognizing and accepting this responsibility, we are free to choose once again—free to choose forgiveness rather than guilt, peace rather than conflict, and free to experience the limitless power of love through the healing of our relationships.

*"Guilt asks for punishment,
and its request is granted."*

LESSON ONE

Forgiveness Heals and Ends the Game of Guilt

To heal is to join and become whole. Healing, therefore, is of the mind, not the body.

Our biggest obstacle to experiencing peace of mind, or oneness with love, is our fear of God. Because we believe we are separate from God, we feel guilty and in conflict and competition with each other—and that is the bottom line of all our difficulties regardless of their nature.

Healing is a process through which our mind is cleansed of its negative thoughts of fear and guilt—all those condemning judgments that make us feel vulnerable, separate, and fragmented. Forgiveness is the means by which this process is accomplished. It permits the mind, that misperceives and sees itself as split and separate, to be made whole.

True healing, therefore, corrects the misperception that our minds are separate from each other and reestablishes our natural state where all minds are joined in love with each other and God. To accomplish healing, it is essential that we constantly remind ourselves that our one purpose in being with another person is to experience joining without judgment.

The Healed Mind

The healed mind does not know the meaning of separateness. Because it contains only God's loving thoughts, it is peaceful and devoid of guilt, pain, and conflict. Its identity is its perfect harmony with the wholeness of love. It does not deny the body, but perceives it as a neutral vehicle for the communication of love without the interference of conflict.

The Game of Guilt

All the conflicting interactions we have with other people, regardless of their forms, are simply variations on the game of guilt. Our ego minds are constantly struggling with the questions: Who is guilty? Who is innocent? With whom are we safe? And, whom are we to fear? Our judgment of guilt is based on interpretations of our past experiences that we introduce and relive in the present. Our ego refuses to acknowledge that whatever we see or hear starts internally—as a thought within our own mind. Since the ego thrives on attack, it will punish by attack whomever it sees as guilty—either ourselves or others. When we no longer see any value in guilt, we can choose to see only the innocence in others as well as in ourselves. When we say good-bye to guilt, we are able to say hello to love.

Mind Controls the Body

The purpose of forgiveness is to heal the mind, not the body. Once we have totally forgiven the other person, and ourselves, and are therefore able to let go of our attack thoughts and guilt, the mind returns to its natural, loving state. The need to suffer is then removed, and the body, following in harmony with the mind, may allow pain and sickness to disappear.

When we are experiencing pain, one of the hardest lessons to learn is that it is not the body that controls the mind, but the mind that controls the body. This lesson is particularly difficult to accept when we have a legitimate organic illness that justifies the reality of our pain.

Mildred's Decision

I had accepted an invitation to give a lecture as part of a two-day conference in another state. The conference director, a woman I shall call Mildred, was scheduled to meet my plane and drive me to the meeting hall—some two hours from the airport.

When I arrived at the airport, however, Mildred was nowhere in sight. As I stood there looking about, a man walked up and said he was Mildred's husband. He explained that Mildred had asked him to meet me because she was suffering from a gallbladder attack that had started a couple of days before. In fact, she was planning to go to the hospital that very afternoon for surgery.

Since it was several hours before my presentation, I asked if it would be possible for me to see Mildred. When we walked in, Mildred greeted us in a weak voice and said she was waiting for a call from her doctor about the availability of a hospital bed. It was obvious she was in severe pain: she appeared pale and greatly distressed.

We talked briefly, and I suggested that she could help herself relax by choosing to put only positive thoughts in her mind and by saying, "I am," whenever she breathed in, and, "relaxed," when she exhaled. After doing this little meditation together for a few minutes, she was able to let go of some of the tension in her body.

I then asked Mildred if she had noticed any unusual stress in her life before the attack started. She responded that, as a matter of fact, she had been quite upset with her employer, a physician for whom she had worked as a receptionist for the past fifteen years.

She went on to explain that he had recently given her permission to redecorate the office—an assignment that gave her great pleasure. She added that she was especially pleased to have the opportunity to take down the "awful" pictures that the physician's sister had put up several years before.

Both Mildred and her employer were happy with their newly decorated space. Shortly after the renovation, however, the physician's sister visited the office and saw that her paintings were no longer on the walls. A confrontation ensued, and, as you may have guessed, the physician sided with his sister and told Mildred that the paintings had to go back up on the wall. Mildred interpreted her boss's reaction as rejection and promptly quit her job.

However, Mildred did not associate this stressful experience with the onset of her gallbladder attack. She saw them as two distinctly separate events. She had denied the guilt she felt about her rage and was unaware that guilt could play a part in the need she felt to punish and attack herself. Instead, she believed her current upset was due to the painful gallbladder attack that prevented her from participating in the conference she had worked so hard on and wanted so much to attend.

I suggested to Mildred that it was possible to change her

GOOD-BYE TO GUILT

belief system. Rather than seeing her former employer as rejecting and attacking, she could, if she chose, see him as fearful and asking for her help. I also reminded her that she didn't have to forgive—she only needed to be willing to forgive—and then her inner teacher, the voice of love, would do the rest.

I took her hands and we prayed together. I did not ask God to remove Mildred's pain. Rather, my prayer was one of gratitude for His presence and the joining that Mildred and I were experiencing with Him. After about twenty minutes of silence, Mildred opened her eyes and said she felt "such peace," and that her pain had totally disappeared.

Shortly thereafter the telephone rang, and Mildred answered it. It was the doctor asking to speak to Mildred. At first, he did not recognize her voice, which was no longer weak and filled with pain, but full of energy and vitality. He was calling to say that a bed was now available for her at the hospital. When Mildred reported that she no longer had any pain and, in fact, felt so well she did not plan to be hospitalized, he was greatly surprised. However, he agreed with her decision and told her to let him know if the pain recurred.

Indeed, Mildred felt well enough to attend the entire two-day conference, and she became a teacher to all of us about the power of the mind over the body. Since that time, we have continued to correspond with each other, and, to date, Mildred has not had a recurrence of her gallbladder problem.

Laura Unlocks the Door to Happiness

Our ego is very skillful at devising ways to insure its survival. And essential to its survival is fear, for without fear the ego would cease to exist. Fear is always based on the perception of being attacked, and the ego's advice to us when we perceive ourselves as being attacked is to be afraid and defensive or attack back.

Laura's letter reminds us that we are never upset for the reason we think, and that healing our relationships depends on forgiveness and letting go of guilt.

Dear Dr. Jampolsky:

I have always been an intensely spiritual being. Born into a Jewish background, I have been equally open to embrace passionately any and every spiritual vehicle that could offer me "nirvana."

In March of 1981, while in the process of an eighteen-month separation from my husband of fifteen years that would eventually culminate in divorce, I found out that my mother had stomach cancer and needed surgery immediately. I flew down to Florida to be with her.

I was also emotionally involved with a man, who, while he was a beautiful person in many ways, was very destructive to my whole sense of being. I was probably even more distraught over this than the possibility of the loss of my mother, whom I "desperately" loved and needed.

To give you some insight into how distraught I was, I was having dreams of my estranged husband, my boyfriend, and my therapist—holding me up high, and Jesus was trying to touch me with his finger tips—but we kept missing each other. I kept resisting. I wasn't ready to give up, but felt everyone wanted me to. I was being crushed. I was self-destructing—fighting death.

I went to see my therapist who, in his eagerness to help, kept telling me that I should be angry at the way everyone was treating me.

I drove to the only peaceful place I knew—a lake—and I began to cleanse my body, my mind—everything was illuminated!!! I began to forgive—to let go—I understood instantly what the word baptism meant—the message behind Yom Kippur—God was forgiving me. All I had to do was forgive everyone else.

I did. I forgave my husband. I forgave my boyfriend—who had his tongue in his cheek as he listened to me.

But it didn't matter then that he didn't believe me because I believed it. I knew it. I was light—I was cleansed—I was reborn. I was peaceful—I was happy.

You showed me how to find forgiveness. You reminded me that when someone is attacking me, it is really not me that is being attacked, but themselves—their fears—their guilt—their own perception of powerlessness. It taught me to love them more because it made me realize that they needed love more. The more a person "attacks," the more he needs love, and the more I should reach out and reassure him.

I still love them both. I can feel their pain. Sometimes I can help them—but I never feel threatened by them anymore.

Two years later this boyfriend came to me and told me that he finally was beginning to realize that I had actually forgiven him—but that he couldn't believe me in 1981 because he wasn't able to forgive himself. Now that he could, he also accepted my unconditional love and forgiveness.

Thank you for helping me unlock the door.

Laura

Author's note: Laura also told me that only hours after her experience of being "reborn," she met a man who was to become her husband two years later. In retrospect she added:

I know now what happened. I was being pre-pared to receive a "gift" from God. I had to end my old life—to make peace with everyone—with myself—with God—to be ready to receive my "gift."

Forgiveness heals and ends the game of guilt.
The world I see through the eyes of guilt and un-forgiveness is indeed a threatening world. Yet, there is another way of looking at this same world. I can choose to look at familiar people and things as though I were seeing them for the first time. Without my guilt and lack of forgiveness from the past, I can experience the beauty, joy, and contentment that lie all around me, and in all the people who are part of my life.

Steps for Integrating Today's Lesson into Our Daily Life Experiences

1. Identify someone with whom you are playing the game of guilt today. Decide to forgive that person for whatever you think he/she may have done to you as you repeat to yourself: *Forgiveness heals and ends the game of guilt.*

2. Think of someone you have not yet forgiven. Say directly to this person today: "Please help me let go of the past and join with me as my brother/sister in love." (If it is not possible to say this directly, repeat it mentally.)

3. Think of a specific goal that you can share with an-other person today. As you work toward that goal,

focus on at least two ways in which you can demonstrate extending love and peace.

4. Make a commitment today to experience joining with one other person—your spouse, your child, your parents, a friend, or colleague—and follow through on your commitment.

5. Repeat throughout the day whenever you experience guilt, fear, or unforgiving thoughts: "This is my instant of releasing you, (*specify name*), and myself from a guilty and unforgiving world. Together we can join in seeing a healed world free from guilt."

*"All anger is nothing more
than an attempt to make someone
feel guilty."*

Choosing Love Offers Me Freedom from Fear

We can choose freedom or bondage. We can choose love, or fear and guilt. Our ego-mind or personality-self does not want us to believe that we have these choices. It tells us that we live in a world where freedom from fear is impossible. It encourages us to believe that fear is not only real, but justified, normal, and healthy. It insists that external situations in our lives are beyond our control, and that when we get caught in these situations, we have no choice but to experience fear. According to our ego, fear is not a choice but an unavoidable part of our experience.

All too frequently, a day in our lives will go by in which, despite our good intentions of being on a spiritual pathway, we choose fear and allow our ego-minds to take over. When this happens to me, it feels as though the world has spent most of the day crushing in on me, causing me great unrest, and leaving me with an apprehensive feeling of fear in my stomach and bones. If anyone dared tell me that the feeling I was experiencing was a choice and not a result of the awful things that were happening to me and beyond my control, I would certainly think that that person didn't really understand what life was all about. Our ego-mind is so deceptive that it wants to convince us that our emotional responses are the result of other people or events outside ourselves, and that they have nothing to do with our internal thoughts.

Choosing Another Way

Another way of looking at the world is to be aware that both love and fear are choices, and that we can train our minds to choose one or the other. In order to do this, we must remind ourselves over and over that it is our belief system that is responsible for what we see—not external situations. It is our own thoughts about these situations that will determine whether we experience peace or conflict, love, or fear. I have found the following quotation from the course most helpful in resisting the temptation to interpret, judge, and become fearful:

"What is not love is always fear, and nothing else."

This concept is so beautifully simple that my ego-mind continues to resist it. Yet there are those times when I am willing to open my heart to the gift of God's love and listen only to His words telling me what to think, say, and do. During those times I am able to experience more and more peace in my life.

As I pray and do my best to listen to God's words, I have never been told to try to change other people or tell them what to do—something I used to think was my function. Instead, my inner voice asks me to "wake up" and recognize the presence of God's light within me, which is shining out to the whole universe and being reflected back. My inner voice has also asked me to acknowledge that as a child of God, I am joined with all others as one Self with no separation.

Spiritual Leaders

Most spiritual leaders who stand out in the history of mankind have shared one thing in common: a total commitment to God and to forgiving the world and everyone in it. My ego-mind used to argue with the often-quoted statement of one such leader, Jesus, that all of us can do what he did in his life and more. It sounded like beautiful rhetoric, but in my heart I really didn't feel it applied to me. How could I ever succeed in being as completely forgiving and nonjudgmental as Jesus?

Rationalization

I realize that almost everyone has felt this way. We would like to accept the possibility that we can be totally forgiving and nonjudgmental, but what we really believe is, "Well, it may work for those relatively few historically acclaimed spiritual leaders, and perhaps for some who have not been so famous, but it certainly will not work for me." And then we rationalize our skepticism by saying that, "After all, things were different when those unusual persons were alive, and the problems we face today are much more complex and difficult."

Yet it is my belief that today's problems are exactly the same as those that people faced thousands of years ago—only their forms are different. The temptation to judge and condemn others, to act like sheep and follow the majority instead of our own inner teacher, to evaluate and separate ourselves into the "innocent" and the "guilty" are the same issues that mankind has always had to face.

Commitment

My commitment to God has certainly not been a steady one, but those moments when I have committed myself, I've experienced a glorious feeling of wholeness and oneness. My mind has felt joined with other minds for the purpose of extending love and joy. When I am feeling angry, I cannot hear the voice of love, the voice of God. I find that I constantly need to remind myself that anger—no matter how justified—never brings me the peace of mind that I want.

Recently I was talking to Mother Teresa and telling her of my wish to learn how to commit and surrender myself totally to God. She was most kind and said I was being too harsh on myself. She went on to explain, "What is important is our intentionality of devoting our lives to God—but living in the world, it is not possible to give our attention to God all of the time. It is the intentionality that counts."

To Give and to Forgive

We can feel the peaceful presence of God when we take one instant at a time and make that a moment only for giving and forgiving—instead of getting and blaming. As we learn to give more and find that giving *is* receiving, we can then see why it is important to let go of our investment in guilt, condemnation, and blame. In doing this, we realize that we must accept responsibility for our freedom and happiness since we can be hurt by nothing but our own thoughts.

It is our own thoughts that determine whether our minds are joined in love with other minds—or whether we are living in a world of separation where we are constantly vulnerable to attack. This perception of our vulnerability to attack is really a defense against experiencing the peace of God.

"Repairing" My Mind

As an example of this, I would like to share with you an experience I had this past year with the telephone company in which I chose to perceive myself as attacked, and, as a result, I experienced guilt, anger, and fear. Every time I think I have forgiven the telephone company, a new challenge seems to arise which tests my "forgiveness quotient."

A few months ago the following episode took place. I had been working at my home where I have two phones. Both phones simultaneously developed static to the degree that I could not hear anything. My secretary called the repair service and, despite their prompt response, two hours later the phones were nonfunctional again. The next day, after a second visit from the repairman, they went out of order again.

This on-again, off-again service continued for a period of two weeks. Each day when I found my phones not working, I became more frustrated and felt justified anger raging inside me. My thoughts regarding this situation were anything but forgiving.

Feeling I was being victimized, and believing my peace of mind depended on my phones working, there was no way that I wanted to think that I could be hurt by nothing but my thoughts. For sure, I thought the telephone company and their incompetent repairmen were the cause of my unhappiness. Any thoughts about God or love completely escaped me.

A week later, after I had given up all hope of resolving my phone problems, a new repairman came to the door. I was just about to give him a piece of my angry mind about the incompetency of the servicemen who had preceded him, when it suddenly dawned on me that my peace of mind did not depend on whether or not my phones functioned properly. It occurred to me that I was setting up a very negative reality for myself, and by continuing to be unforgiving, I was only going to cause myself more distress. (How stubborn and deceptive our ego-mind can be!)

What I decided to do was to leave him with the phones, go to my desk, and concentrate only on sending him unconditional love. I tried to see only the light of God's love in him and not to believe that my peace of mind depended on whether my phones got fixed.

About forty minutes later the repairman came over to me and said the phones were now in working order. I thanked him, and then he went on to say that he had seen me on television a few times talking about attitudinal healing and could I please tell him a little more about it. As I began to explain to him some of the principles of attitudinal healing, I found myself discussing more and more how important forgiveness is in learning how to heal our attitudes. I couldn't help but be amused by the irony of this situation—here I was trying to teach someone about forgiveness when I badly needed to learn more about it myself! Before he left, I offered him a copy of my book, *Love Is Letting Go of Fear*, which seemed to please him.

The following day the phones went out of order, and my secretary once again called the repair service. That night when I came home, there was a printed form that the telephone man had been there, along with a personal note. To my amazement, it was from the same repairman who had been there the previous day.

That was the first miracle—they sent the same man back two days in a row! But there were miracles in the personal note as well. The first paragraph stated that he had finally located the problem with my phones, and this time they were really fixed. The second paragraph stated that if anything should go wrong with my phones in the future, I was to call the supervisor—and he gave me his name and phone number—who would contact him directly about making the necessary repairs.

Then the third paragraph had another miracle in it. He said that if, for any reason, I could not reach the supervisor, I could call him at his home, and he supplied me with his home phone number. Now have any of you ever heard of a telephone repairman leaving his own personal phone number? An additional surprise was that he signed the note, "Love, Robert." There was also a P.S.: "Your book is marvelous. It changed at least some of the world for me."

This experience became a very powerful lesson to me. It became very clear that by changing the thoughts in my mind, the reality I saw changed. And I realized with great clarity that if I had pursued my angry and unforgiving thoughts, I would have continued to be in conflict. My goal became to claim my freedom by deciding to choose love instead of fear.

As a way of not forgetting this valuable experience—of reminding myself that I can only be hurt by my thoughts—I had the note from Robert framed where it remains on my living room wall. There was a second hidden reason for framing his note—I don't want to lose his number!

Choosing love offers me freedom from fear. *Most of my life I responded automatically to what other people said or did. Now I recognize that my responses can be determined only by the decisions I make. I claim my freedom by exercising the power of my decision to see people and events with love instead of fear.*

Steps for Integrating Today's Lesson into Our Daily Life Experiences

1. Let me recognize that whatever feelings I experience today—peace or love, or some form of fear (anger, depression, etc.)—are determined by the thoughts I put into my mind. I choose to hold on to only the thoughts I want.

2. Remind yourself hourly today that choosing love offers freedom from fear. Be determined to claim your freedom and let thoughts of love replace all your fear.

3. When you think things are going wrong in your life today, stop for a moment and say to yourself, "It is not other people or events that cause me to be unhappy. I can choose peace instead of this."

4. Since I know that I can be hurt only by my own thoughts, I will resist the temptation today to blame others. Instead, I claim the opportunity to see myself and everyone else as free from guilt and fear.

5. Review the summary of this lesson at least twice today: *choosing love offers me freedom from fear.*

*"The guiltless mind cannot
suffer."*

LESSON THREE

I Will Not Hurt
Myself Again Today*

Basic to the ego's thought system is the belief that the external world is the cause of our pain. It is not unusual for many of us to awaken in the morning with the fearful thought, "What awful thing is going to happen to me today?" Our newspapers as well as radio and television broadcasts constantly bombard us with reports of events that reinforce the feeling that we live in a very unsafe world and are continuously vulnerable to some form of attack.

Since the world's belief system makes it seem impossible for us to just "let go and trust," most of us feel that sooner or later we are doomed to experience pain and despair. Our ego-mind—which is another name for this belief system—has made things very complicated. Its motto is, "Seek, but never find what you are looking for." By encouraging us to become fault-finders and judgment-makers, the ego blocks our awareness of the very love we seek.

*A Course in Miracles, Workbook, Lesson 330.

In truth, love and attack cannot coexist, although the ego would have us believe they can. Therefore, when we fail to find the happiness we seek, the ego convinces us that our fear, guilt, and unhappiness are caused by some external condition or person.

As long as we continue to look at the world in this way, we will feel hurt over and over again and be unable to experience peace of mind on a consistent basis. If we are to free ourselves from a belief system that perceives fear and guilt as real, we must be willing and determined to see things differently.

World of God

Contrasted with God's world of love, the ego's thought system is clearly upside down. For in the world of God, love is the only reality there is, and it is impossible for us to experience any fear or guilt. When we are practicing the law of love, we choose to let each thought and action be an extension of God's love. In doing this, we make the decision to become love-finders rather than fault-finders. And in making this decision, we choose not to respond in judgment to anyone or anything in our external world.

Change in Perception

The times I am most happy and peaceful are the moments when I remember that the only thing that is real in my mind is the light of Christ, the light of God. And when I forget this and make judgments about something or someone, I become miserable. I feel attacked because I have forgotten that the perception of being attacked originates in my own mind. My own attack thoughts simply act like boomerangs that come back to hit me.

There is a statement from *A Course in Miracles* that I have found personally helpful in my efforts to see things differently:

> *Today I let Christ's vision look upon*
> *All things for me and judge them not, but give*
> *Each one a miracle of love instead.*

This statement reminds me that everything I see is determined by the thoughts I put in my mind. When I choose to have only God's thoughts in my mind, there is only the extension of love—there is no projection, there is no judgment.

Healing Our Wounds

Immediately following my divorce, I seemed to become even more attached to the ego's way of looking at the world. As I saw it, the world was based on personal guilt, loss, rejection, and deprivation of love. I felt wounded and unlovable. Furthermore, I had a need to prove that I was unlovable. I did not trust women—and, more important, I certainly did not trust myself.

About a year and a half after my divorce, I deceived myself into believing that my wounds had been healed. I began to feel more in control of my life and that it was safe for me to trust my feelings once again. It was about this time that I met a woman who was attractive, intelligent, and stable—all the things I thought I was not. What I lacked, I felt she had, and through her, I could achieve a sense of completion. In the excitement of our intense attraction for one another, we convinced ourselves that we were partners in a relationship made in heaven. Even though I believed I'd found peace in this relationship, I continued to drink excessively.

Later, I learned that any relationship based on need or a

misperceived lack in oneself is actually based on hate. What we call love in relationships of this kind is really the illusion of love, which covers up the hate we feel about our own sense of incompleteness.

While I was still strongly under the spell of this illusory love, another man came into the picture. Although I felt I was being deceived by my partner, I was uncertain about the details. When we finally confronted this situation and my worst fears were confirmed, my ego had a field day. My old feelings of being unlovable, inadequate, and unwanted took over again. No one could have convinced me that I was not being hurt by both my partner and her new lover. It was impossible for me to believe then that only my own thoughts could hurt me.

When we allow our ego mind to take over, particularly in our romantic relationships, feelings of jealousy and possessiveness consume us. We believe the person we love is causing us to feel pain. When that person devotes an inordinate amount of time and attention to someone else who seems more entertaining or interesting than we think we are, our so-called love turns into hate. When the person we love no longer wants to have a close relationship with us, but wants to have an intimate relationship with a new person, we are devastated.

The ego keeps telling us that we are being hurt by the other person, and that our anger is justified. The ego would have us remain vulnerable for the rest of our life with the fear that this could happen again if we allow ourselves to become close to someone. The ego teaches us that we cannot trust another person, we cannot trust ourselves, and we cannot even trust God. It would have us believe that the past will repeat itself, and that our security rests on remaining unforgiving.

It took a long time for me to recognize that no one could hurt me but myself. It was only my own thoughts and attitudes that were hurtful. Lack of trust and self-deception were my own internal problems, which I projected onto others.

When I finally took responsibility for my own thoughts and saw both my partner and her lover as guiltless, I was able, through forgiveness, to let go of the past and the misperception that I had been wronged. My relationship with both parties then became healed.

More and more I have come to recognize the crucial importance of committing each day to joy, rather than to suffering. Without guilt, there is no need to hurt myself again. As I look back on that experience, I can recognize now that it was really a love-hate relationship. When our needs are satisfied by another, we feel love; and if they are not satisfied, we are likely to feel hate. The moment we want something from another person, we give that person the power to decide whether or not we will be happy. We give them the power to hurt us.

If we feel that others are causing us to feel pain, frustration, or hate, it simply means that we are using that relationship to block off the awareness of God's presence within us. This special relationship is one that is based on ego needs and illusions, in contrast to a holy relationship in which both persons' wills are joined and given over to God. In one sense, all relationships are special. They are used to develop idols of love or idols of hate as a substitute for God. Most of us have great resistance to putting God first in all our relationships. Yet, if we are to find consistent peace, it is exactly this commitment we must make.

We must be willing to relinquish our ego needs and see them for what they really are—illusions. Once again, we need to awaken to the truth that there is no separation, that we are always joined in God's love, that His will for us is perfect happiness, and that we are complete and whole with no lack or need.

When we feel hurt, it is because we have identified with others' bodies as their reality—rather than recognizing their true reality lies in the nonphysical essence of love.

Victim of the Universe

Recently I received a letter from a woman named Janie Peto that describes the joy that we can experience when we are willing to let go of the guilty past and our condemning judgments of others and ourselves.

Dear Dr. Jampolsky,

I just finished reading your article, written with Patricia Hopkins, in the February issue of *UNITY* Magazine.

I was restless, moody, depressed, ready to freak out with worry or just to go to bed. I paced, then went directly to the magazine, opened to your article, read it through, and the tears just poured out. God! How I've been punishing myself! I've been a failure in God's eyes because he was looking through mine! If nothing is impossible then maybe I can rescue myself after all!

Briefly, I've been on a search for "treatment" all my life for nerves, depression, guilt, phobias— the works. I was convinced that I was born "the victim of the universe." I always attracted losers, beaters, and painmakers. I have never had a true relationship. About ten years ago, I checked out and became a hermit. I thought love was only in the movies.

Then last June, God opened a door for me. He sent me my soulmate. Because of his past hurts and my own dark pain, our relationship began slowly—and hurtfully. I always expected the worst.

Through prayer, I've been able to "hang onto"

this man for the past year and improve our relationship ten times over! I share light with him, and we are becoming human beings again! I'm just so happy right now that I could scream!

Right after reading your words, my friend called me and set up a date! Thanks to you, I can lift myself higher—because I got closer to the truth! I keep dropping back into fear and the "pits," so when something inspiring like this happens to me, I turn myself around again! I can believe! I can hope! What a fantastic feeling!

My problem is small compared to all that's going on on our planet, but, Dr. Jampolsky, the ray of sunshine you sent this little soul was appreciated in a big way!

Thank you!
God bless you!
Love & Light,

(signed) *Janie Peto*

"I will not hurt myself again today" means being determined not to see illusions having any effect, and reminding ourselves that we can only be hurt by our own thoughts. When we recognize that our only true relationship is with God—and that it is a love relationship that is always perfectly complete and fulfilling—we will never feel empty again. And we can then see the God-self in all others. By continuing to give our love away, we will find that we have increasingly more love than we did before.

As we begin to know with certainty that our true reality is love, we will also know that nothing real can be threatened and that nothing unreal exists.

I will not hurt myself again today. *I recognize today that my attack thoughts about others are really di-*

rected against myself. When I believe that attacking others brings me something I want, let me remember that I always attack myself first.

Steps for Integrating Today's Lesson into Our Daily Life Experiences

1. Review your relationships and select the one(s) in which you feel most vulnerable to hurt or pain. Now recognize that you can hurt yourself only by your own thoughts. Then say to yourself, "I am determined not to attack myself again. (*Specify name*), I choose to experience only love instead of pain in my relationship with you today."

2. Let go today, if only for a moment, of the belief that anyone has the power to hurt you. Instead, say to whomever you feel threatened by, "I see you joined with me in the light of God's healing love."

3. Reaffirm your willingness to see only the God-self in everyone you meet today. Imagine that you are wearing a "love filter" over your eyes and ears. Be open to seeing and hearing only loving faces and words today.

4. If you feel that your peace of mind is being threatened in any relationship today say to yourself, "I will not use you (*specify name*) to block my awareness of God's presence in both of us."

5. At least three times today, repeat the following affirmation: "Since I am surrounded and protected by the love of God, I choose not to hurt myself again today."

*"The guiltless have no fear,
for they are safe and
recognize their safety."*

LESSON FOUR

Let Me Not See
Myself As Limited

I do not think it can be repeated too often that whatever we see or hear, whatever emotions we experience, originate in the thoughts that we, ourselves, put into our minds. Our illusions about ourselves and our illusions about the world we see are one and the same.

When we are upset, we see ourselves as limited and feel like victims of the world we live in. Yet our upsets have nothing to do with the external world. They are simply the reflections of our own thoughts. Although I say this with great conviction, I must confess to you that each day I am tempted to believe that what I see and hear in the world around me is real—and I am not always successful in resisting this temptation.

Perception Is a Choice

Our ego does not want us to believe that it is not our own thoughts that hurt us. It does not want us to believe that what we see and hear is only a projection of our own thoughts that keep us separate and limited. Most of all, our ego does not want us to believe that perception is a choice and not a fact. The ego is so clever in disguising this that we fall into the trap of believing that we are the victims of our own perceptions. The only thing that can rescue us is the concept of forgiveness. For it is through forgiveness that we are able to remove the limits we have imposed and see the light in ourselves and in others.

Our ego-mind has very ingenious and devious techniques for blocking us from taking responsibility for our own thoughts. For instance, it encourages us to make evaluations and interpretations so we can justify fear and the perceptions of pain and anguish; it wants us to have doubts and uncertainties. Its enemy is peace. Through its use of deception, it would have us believe that all of our upsets and unhappiness are caused by other people or external conditions. It tries to persuade us that if someone would only act differently or a situation would change, all of our problems would disappear.

The Ego's Plan for Survival

The concept of timelessness is beyond the ego's comprehension. On the contrary, it requires us to accept as real a world whose existence depends on the past, present, and future. Furthermore, it fosters the illusion that we are limited in the present by what happened in the past and will likely recur in the future.

In order for the ego to survive, it is necessary for us to believe that we are separate from all other minds and limited to the dimensions of our physical bodies. Its plan for survival is based on holding grievances against separate bodies, and its reality is a world of fragmentation and separation, where we are limited by guilt and fear, and love is lacking.

It is up to us whether we want to live in God's world or the world of the ego. It is up to us to choose which voice we want to hear. We can be conscious of each instant as a moment in which we can awaken and experience God's eternal love, or we can choose to believe we are limited and imprisoned by our own self-created ego from which there is no escape.

Release from the Prison of Guilt

Recently I was given a book that contained the following quotation from Tolstoy. I feel it captures the essence of today's lesson in a very poetic way.

> Jesus Christ teaches men that there is something in them which lifts them above this life with its hurries, its pleasures and fears. He who understands Christ's teaching feels like a bird who did not know it had wings—and now suddenly realizes it can fly, can be free, and no longer needs to fear.

We *are* lifted up when we decide to live in that moment where there is no time or space, and where the only vision we use is Christ's Light, which joins us in love and oneness with each other and God. We are free of all limits when we are not imprisoned by guilt.

Passing the Test

In 1980, after having been a student of *A Course in Miracles* for five years, I became very fearful when I was suddenly faced with a crisis in my life. At the time, my fears seemed very justified and real to me. In fact, I was in a state of panic and in this frame of mind I decided to stop studying the course.

What had happened was this: I had just returned from a speaking tour and my secretary, after welcoming me back, asked me to sit down as she had some bad news for me. That was an understatement! What she proceeded to tell me was that I did not have a current medical license, and, moreover, according to state records I had not been licensed to practice medicine in California since 1973! I couldn't believe what I was hearing.

After several days, and what later seemed like hundreds of frantic telephone calls, I learned the cause of this dilemma. In 1973, the State Board of Medical Quality Assurance had neglected to mail out some three hundred bills for license renewals and mine had been among them. However, since I did not know this at the time, I just assumed the bill had arrived, the annual fee had been paid as usual by my bookkeeper, and everything was in order. Unfortunately, this was not the case, and my license had been dropped.

Although this explained why I was now in this unenviable situation, the fact was that failure to renew the license was my responsibility—bill or no bill—and in order to be reinstated by the board, I was informed it would be necessary for me to take the state qualifying examination again. The last time I had taken this exam was in 1949, more than thirty years ago, and I was no longer even vaguely familiar with the material I would be expected to know in order to pass.

Since I had never done well on exams in the past—and there was no reason to believe this time would be an exception—I was very worried. In addition, with all of my other responsibilities, I didn't see how I could find the time to study. I thought the world was out to get me by limiting my ability to function professionally. I hardly needed anyone to tell me I was a victim; I had no doubt about that!

The exam was to be an oral one administered by two physicians. I was convinced that with my first response, they would discover how incompetent I was, and I would never see my license again. I was sure they intended to make mincemeat out of me, and that it wouldn't take them very long to do it.

After indulging in these fearful projections for a few weeks, I began to realize that the way I had chosen to handle this situation was not working. It was *not* giving me peace of mind. I decided to resume my daily study of the course.

As I began to meditate and ask for guidance, I became aware that the doctors who would be examining me were not out to get me; they were there to help me. My inner voice told me not to see them as enemies but as my brothers—my friends. The voice also directed me to study for two months before taking the exam, but not to be concerned about any material I was unable to cover within that time. I began to forgive the world, and, gradually, I was able to perceive what I was going through as a positive lesson God would have me learn.

Instead of staying up all night before the test and cramming, as I used to do when I was in medical school, I went to bed early. The next day I arrived an hour early at the place where I was to be examined in order to compose myself and pray. I did not pray that I would pass the test, but rather for peace of mind and seeing myself as one with the examiners and God.

Well, a first-class miracle occurred: I passed the exam! And in the process I learned I did not have to choose to see myself as a victim or as limited in any way.

*   *   *

I am beginning to understand that everything that happens to me—no matter how horrendous it seems at the time—can be turned into a positive learning experience. I've also learned that experiences that are helpful to me can assist others who are having similar problems.

For example, not long ago, I was giving a workshop on healing relationships at a university. During a dialogue with members of the audience, a second-year medical student, whom I shall call Bob, related the following story. A year ago, Bob had been dropped from medical school because of his abuse of alcohol and drugs. In two days he was going to appear before a review committee of the school to determine whether or not he could be reinstated, and he was afraid the hearing would result in a negative judgment against him.

I shared my story about losing my license and reminded Bob that he, too, could choose to look upon the members of the review committee as his friends. I emphasized that it was important for him to decide that his peace of mind was not contingent on the outcome of the hearing. I suggested that his purpose in life is not to see others as threatening, but rather to see them as kind, gentle, and loving. Many people in the audience befriended Bob that day, and some stayed in touch with him by phone after the conference was over.

Two days later Bob appeared before the review committee. Afterward he reported he had felt peaceful during the proceedings, but he would still have to wait several weeks for the decision. Six weeks later, Bob called to tell me that he had, indeed, been reinstated. He added that his motivation for being in medical school had changed—now he truly wanted to serve others, without the limits imposed by his former addictions.

Spiritual Speed

Sister Marion Irvine is the principal of San Francisco's Sacred Heart Grammar School in the heart of the city's Western Addition, an area that has a reputation for being a tough neighborhood. Six years ago at the age of forty-eight, she was persuaded by a niece—who wanted to lose weight—to join her for a run, and Sister Marion has been running ever since. Today, at the age of fifty-four, she holds American records for her age group (50–54) in all the standard distances from five kilometers up to the marathon. Recently, she became the oldest person ever to qualify for the Olympic trials in an endurance race.

At the time Sister Marion decided to become a runner, she weighed nearly two hundred pounds and smoked over two packs of cigarettes a day. Today, a confirmed nonsmoker, she maintains an ideal weight for running. She also had a thirty-year history of what she refers to as a sedentary lifestyle. Despite her history, Sister Marion did not allow her past belief system to impose limits on her present or future potential. And when the mind knows no limitations, the body can respond in a truly amazing way.

Sister Marion believes that running is a good time for being reflective and for praying. She describes it as "a kind of harmonizing of the physiology with the environment. It's especially elevating and humbling at the same time. Running along a beach at sunrise with no other footprints on the sand, you realize the vastness of creation, your own insignificant space in that plan, . . . your own creatureliness, and how much you owe to the Supreme Body, the God that brought all this beauty and harmony into being. It's really some of the most exhilarating prayer time I experience."

In addition to her full-time responsibilities as a school administrator, Sister Marion still finds time to run at least ten miles daily and plans to continue her marathon running in national as well as international competitions. Her achievements are a beautiful reminder to all of us that advancing age does not preclude women—or men—from seeking and succeeding at new adventures. When we join our will with God's, there are no limits.

Be resolved today to place no limits on your potential as you say:

Let me not see myself as limited. *I can preoccupy myself with fears of past limitations projected onto the future, but I can live only in this present moment. This moment is precious because it is different from all other moments. While the opportunity for my personal growth and fulfillment exists at all times, there has never been a better moment than now. There has never been a better place than here.*

Steps for Integrating Today's Lesson into Our Daily Life Experiences

1. Remind yourself repeatedly today whenever you are tempted to feel guilty or live in the past or future: "I can live here and now with no fear of limitation."

2. Think of one area in your life where you are tempted to see yourself as limited by what you think other people have done or do to you . Remind yourself that perception is a choice—not a fact.

3. Remind yourself that what you see outside is a reflection of what you first see within your own mind. Choose today to have only boundless, loving thoughts in your mind. Choose today to see yourself as unlimited.

4. Review this thought frequently today: "As I change my mind about myself today, I realize that God created me without limits. Now I can see the world differently by recognizing I am not a victim."

5. Repeat throughout the day whenever you are tempted to see yourself as limited: "Only my loving thoughts are real. It is only these I would have in this situation (*specify*) or with this person (*specify name*)."

"See no one, then, as guilty,
and you will affirm the truth
of guiltlessness unto yourself."

LESSON FIVE

Let Peace Replace All My Fear Thoughts Today

In today's world, many of us feel that being able to experience peace of mind is simply a matter of chance or good luck. This assumption is based on our investment in all the fears we have been subjected to in our past. Even though we may not be consciously aware of it, most of us are attracted to the pain, anxiety, and guilt we believe we have experienced as a result of these fears. Our belief system is so cleverly constructed that it has succeeded in hoodwinking us. We actually believe that if we are *not* experiencing distress, something must be wrong!

Resistance to Peace

The philosophy I have just described was faithfully practiced in my family circle, where each day we anticipated the tide of terror that tomorrow would bring. As a follower of this belief system for most of my life, I can testify that it hardly encourages one to believe it is possible to find peace or joy in the present moment.

A Course in Miracles states that one of the goals of the ego-self is the desire to get rid of peace. In others words, although we may consciously think we want peace, if we hold on to guilt, there is another part of our mind that is not only unwilling to accept, but actually resists peace.

Peace of mind is the proclaimed enemy of the ego-self. What keeps the ego-self alive and well nourished is our attachment to guilt, fear, anger, and attack. The ego believes that justified anger is more important and more valuable than peace of mind; it believes that attack is real, and that by defending ourselves, we can have peace of mind. The ego wants to murder and destroy; the ego wants death.

Peace Is a Choice

We need to remind ourselves that peace or conflict is always our choice. We are truly responsible for what we experience. Peace does not come to us by chance or good luck. Peace or conflict always come from a decision we have made ourselves—a decision to put into our minds only loving thoughts, or a decision to hold on to thoughts that are fearful, judgmental, and attacking.

As an illustration of the conflict and exhaustion we create for ourselves when our minds become what I describe as "overloaded" with judgmental thoughts, I would like to share a personal story with you.

Several years ago I was asked by a company to become a member of its board of directors. At first, I was ambivalent about accepting the invitation, but finally I agreed to do so.

A few weeks later, I attended my first board meeting. As

I sat listening to the minutes of the previous meeting being read, I found myself becoming more and more upset, and making more and more judgments. As the meeting progressed, I became increasingly distressed about the kinds of decisions board members were expected to make. Although I was not fully conscious of it at the time, I realized later that I spent most of the session finding fault with someone or something. And when I was not being critical, I concentrated on being bored. When I finally arrived home later that evening, I was totally exhausted. (Recently I have become convinced that most fatigue and exhaustion come from the energy we expend making judgments against ourselves and others.)

The following day, meditating on the conflict I had felt during the meeting, it became clear to me that, as I listened to the minutes being read, I had made a decision to judge who was guilty and who was innocent. And in making the decision to be judgmental, I chose to experience conflict.

Before the next board meeting, I meditated on choosing peace instead of the conflict I had previously chosen. I pictured myself as a battery sending out only positive energy to everyone in the room, and I made a decision to do my best to be a love-finder rather than a fault-finder. During the meeting, I made no comments or statements. I simply listened attentively to what was being discussed. At the end of the meeting, I felt peaceful, and I knew that the feeling of peace was no accident; I had chosen it.

Then an amazing thing happened. Before leaving, two of the board members came to me individually and thanked me for the helpful comments I had made, although, as I mentioned earlier, I had not opened my mouth once during the entire meeting! What I believe occurred was that they felt my love and support and wanted to acknowledge it in some way, so they thanked me for my unspoken remarks.

This was a very beautiful learning experience for me. It demonstrated to me, once again, that when you extend unconditional love, you experience the truth that minds are joined. We can *choose* to experience peace rather than conflict, fear, and guilt.

A Crisis of Fear

I would like to share with you a rather dramatic letter from a woman named Judi. In it she describes how difficult it has been for her to experience peace because of a traumatic incident that occurred in her life, and how the fears surrounding this incident from her past kept intruding into her present life.

Dear Jerry,

On July 6, 1980, I was folding my laundry in the laundry room of our apartment building when a man entered. As the room is usually locked and only tenants have keys, I thought little of it until I sensed he was coming "too close" to me and that he had a knife. He threatened to kill me if I screamed and then lunged at me with the knife, wounding me slightly on the chest. I began to run and to scream for help. The rest is a jumble. I know he slashed at me, and I fell backwards against some storage lockers. He wounded me once again (this wound the most severe). It seemed to happen in slow motion. I remember feeling like it was all just a movie and that even though I had already been hurt, I somehow couldn't believe that the man or the knife could really hurt me. Suddenly he was retreating out the door he had entered (left unlocked by someone who had forgotten her change).

I picked myself up and ran out the door and up to our apartment. My husband called the police.

Looking back, I can laugh at myself. I wanted to appear as calm as possible for my two-year-old, but I refused to sit down lest I bleed on our furniture. The police came instantly. As they questioned me, I complained that they had left our front door open, and I worried that our cat would escape. It was then pointed out to me that I could have been killed—an idea that had never occurred to me.

My description of the man was vague—only an impression of a sweep of blond bangs, a square-shaped face, and eyes full of hate. Later on, looking through mug shots of sex offenders (as the police classified the crime though no rape occurred), I had a physical reaction to a face, but this person proved to have an alibi. It ended there.

Anyway, after questioning, I was taken to the hospital, cared for, and released. In shock, we drove to my parents' home and wound up staying there for the rest of the summer.

I was raised sort of Jewish, observing the holidays and eating the traditional foods, but there was no emotional support there. My parents could not (and still can't) deal with what happened. They provided us with a place to live, but couldn't encourage me to talk to them. (They have hidden it away and won't look at it—or share in my joy now. But I know the potential for this is there.)

In a book I was reading recently, I came across the concept that you create what happens to you with your thoughts. This staggered me, and I longed to know if I had done this thing to myself. I know now I have always been "on the path"—only I didn't see it there already under my feet.

In a swift succession of miracles, as soon as we decided to move (symbolically represented by buying a new house, something we had put off until "some day"), we found our house, the money came to us, and the woman selling the house invited me to attend her prayer/meditation group. I went and kept on going back and have developed a strong bond with these people.

A member of this group invited me to hear you speak at Unity. The title of your talk (as of your book, *Love Is Letting Go of Fear*), leaped out at me. That it was possible to let go of all fear was amazing enough to me, but to fill the void it left with love seemed a miracle.

That night as you shared your story, with humor and gentleness, I felt connected, I felt a love-bond, with you, with the audience, with myself. I knew I would make it. Although my mind didn't understand much of what you said, my heart heard you and rejoiced. I bought your book and left on cloud nine.

Since then I look upon my attack as a crisis of fear, an attack, if you will, of myself on my old way of "not-being." Toward the man involved, from the moment it happened, I felt a curious distance, a sense of impersonality (behind the fear) as though he were an actor playing the role. A friend suggested that perhaps he chose to act out his karma with a soul who would not hold him tied to this action. This thought blew my mind and made me feel very holy, very special, and loved. I feel I didn't forgive him, in a way it wasn't necessary, as if he came to the event forgiven. I didn't blame him; I came to blame myself. I was afraid I would cause it to happen again.

I had been working with your yellow-balloon release idea. I kept stuffing the whole event into the balloon, but I never got it to stay launched. One day it occurred to me to put all the fear in the balloon. Away it sailed into the white light, leaving me free to examine what was left. In came the crashing realization that if I *had* caused my attack, it was all in my power. I could choose not to have it happen again.

With this came the birth of my sense of responsibility for what happens to me. Thoughts held with emotion create. I could choose love over fear.

As I've worked with these concepts I've found a peace and a sense of beauty I would never have dreamed possible. The limitless scope of human possibilities for growth and joy send my heart flying. I feel the connection with my fellow humans. I see the beauty in them, the love we can share. I find myself grinning and giggling and hugging a lot. It is a true miracle.

I want to share further one special section in your book, *Love Is Letting Go of Fear,* about "Attack and Defense." I struggled with that section for a long time. This section might as well have had my name on it for the way it called to me. Finally the light burst through my clouds. I realized the love needed here was for myself. I could release my tight controls. I was terrified to let the real me out. I feared it capable of unspeakable things. Now I know I was afraid the real me was unlovable—a reality more horrible than discovering a monster—indeed someone not worthy of participating in the vital human bond of love would be a monster. I never dreamed of the kind of love I now feel of "Poppa-God" for his dear children.

I learned to dare to try for love, to release my human standards of conduct and perfection for myself. My judgment is harsh and cruel. I am learning to see with my Divine Self, to know that God looks at me and sees His own perfection.

Jerry, thank you for this opportunity to review

what I've experienced and to affirm my own growth.

> Peace be with you.
> Love,
> (signed) *Judi*

In choosing to let go of her past, Judi also learned how to let peace replace all her fear thoughts. We can all make a similar decision for ourselves as we review the following and choose to have a new perception of ourselves and the world.

Let peace replace all my fear thoughts today. *The world transformed through my loving vision shows me that there is nothing to fear. It is impossible for me to experience love and fear at the same time. It is also impossible for me to experience peace when I am fearful. Let peace replace all my fear thoughts today.*

Steps for Integrating Today's Lesson into Our Daily Life Experiences

1. At least once today quiet your mind. Ask yourself if you are resisting peace by holding on to guilt in any form. Remind yourself that when you are fearful of the past and worried about the future, you are choosing not to be at peace.

2. Throughout the day remind yourself that peace of mind is always a choice by repeating the following affirmation: "Today, I choose to experience only

peace by reminding myself: THERE IS NOTHING
TO FEAR."

3. Whenever you feel that your peace is threatened by
   anyone or anything today, stop for a second and
   concentrate on giving all your love to someone.
   Think of nothing else but giving, and you will be at
   peace.

4. Remind yourself that God created you in His im-
   age—free of conflict and perfectly peaceful. As you
   affirm that you are at one with Him, let go of all
   thoughts of separation and recognize that you *are* at
   peace.

5. Be determined to experience only God's love today
   as you hourly affirm: *Let peace replace all my fear
   thoughts today.*

*"Who transcends the body
has transcended limitation."*

LESSON SIX

Through Healed Vision I Know There Is No Death

It is my belief that the greatest fear any of us experiences on earth—either consciously or unconsciously—is the fear of death. As long as we persist in believing that our reality is limited to what we perceive through our physical senses, we will identify with our personality-selves and bodies. As a result we will be tempted to believe that the body and life are one and the same, and when the body dies, life is snuffed out.

True Identity

Healed vision means that we no longer identify ourselves as limited to a physical body, but recognize that our true identity is nonphysical. We are spiritual beings sustained by an everlasting love that never dies.

When we recognize that death is only an illusion, and accept the truth that life and love are eternal, our relationships are dramatically healed. When we truly know this, the illusion of separation vanishes, and we see ourselves as one with the universal mind.

Pause for a moment. Imagine just for one second that you truly believe that death is only an illusion and eternal love is your only reality. For just this one second, imagine that you are joined with all living things, with life and with God, forever. Experience the peace, the quiet, the stillness, the limitless love surrounding you.

Releasing Guilt

Now, look at your relationships and see how quickly the grudges, grievances, and unforgiving thoughts you held a few minutes ago have disappeared. By releasing our fear of death, we are also able to let go of guilt and thereby truly heal our relationships.

Our ego, which we made up, is the great deceiver. On the one hand, it tells us that our bodies are our only reality, and therefore death is to be feared. On the other hand, it hides our fear of death from us in the magical hope that death of the body can be avoided.

The Ego's Secret Teaching

Of all the things our ego-mind attempts to keep hidden from our awareness, three items are at the top of the list:

1. There is no death.

2. There is no separation.

3. There is only love.

The ego has constructed a seemingly impenetrable barrier behind which these truths are hidden. When we retrain our minds to accept the truth of these statements, we will realize that all of our past suffering was a mistake, and that we can choose never to suffer again.

For the ego to stay alive, it must work steadfastly and intently to encourage us to believe that our reality is limited to our physical senses—essentially to what our physical eyes and ears tell us about the world. It would have us believe that there is death, separation, guilt, fear, and hate, and that love is not our reality. The ego-mind is fully aware that as soon as we believe—with total conviction—that there is no death, there is no separation, and there is only love, it will be dissolved.

The Ego vs. God

Is it possible that the great amounts of time and energy we spend trying to control and manipulate others and predict the future are only unconscious displacements of our attempt to control and, thus, deny our fear of death? Is this the ego's way of playing God—feeling that it, instead of God, creates, directs, and controls the universe?

One of the basic lessons in *A Course in Miracles* states that we are "never upset for the reason we think." It suggests that the bottom line of fear we all have, regardless of its form, is the guilt we experience in feeling separate from God and, therefore, from each other. And it is this guilt that leads to our fear of punishment from God in the form of death.

The fear of death is simply an invention of our ego. Being fearful of God, the ego wants us to believe that God is vengeful and, in time, will punish us for our sins. As if this were not threatening enough, it suggests that even more punishment will be meted out to us in hell after we die! The ego's thought system is not only dominated by fear and guilt, but filled with despair and hopelessness as well.

Fear of Death

As mentioned earlier, the fear of death can be on either a conscious or unconscious level. For example, I know people who, while denying that the thought of death is upsetting to them, always turn to the obituary section of the newspaper before reading anything else. It is as if they need to do this in order to assure themselves that they are still alive. These people are usually preoccupied with guilt and unconsciously feel a great need to punish themselves.

I, too, have been afraid of death for most of my life, although I did my best to conceal it from myself, as well as from others. As a physician, I prided myself on my objectivity in dealing with dying patients. Under the guise that the more objective I was, the more helpful I could be, I maintained an emotional distance between myself and terminally ill patients. In retrospect, my "objectivity" was only a way of protecting myself. It was simply a vain attempt on my part to hide the fact that someday that dying patient was going to be me. And since I believed that death was finite, the fear of it was overwhelming to me. However, I kept this hidden from my awareness, tightly locked in one of the many compartments of my mind.

Vision of Love

When we choose to look at the world through the vision of love, in contrast to the ego's orientation, our belief in guilt and death comes to an end. We no longer confuse our identity with our bodies but, instead, recognize the everlasting essence of our spiritual being.

Since being on a spiritual pathway, I am grateful beyond words for the powerful learning experiences I have had from working with families facing death. More and more, I have seen my old fear of death vanishing. It is one thing, however, to deal with the families of the dying, and quite another to apply spiritual principles in your own life—especially when you are faced with the death of someone in your immediate family. Perhaps that is the acid test.

About three years ago at the age of ninety-two, my father died of pneumonia. He had been ill for some time and was quite ready to make his transition. Several weeks before his death, I left for a long trip through the Far East. Thinking it was possible that he might die while I was away, we spent some time together before I left, saying our good-byes to each other. Since I felt that our relationship had been a long and loving one—complete in every way—I truly thought I had released him.

When I arrived in Thailand, I learned of my father's death. At the time, I shed no tears of sadness. I was happy that he had let go and was at peace.

About six months later, while writing an article for a magazine, I described a childhood episode that occurred when I was about three years old. Our family had gone for a Sunday drive, and I had fallen asleep on the way home. I remembered being carried from the car by my dad. I recalled opening my eyes just for one second and then closing them. But for that one second I experienced feelings of comfort, security, love, and, most of all, the complete trust that my father's love would protect me always.

As I finished writing about that memory, I burst into tears. At that moment, I had identified with the body, and I missed my father's physical presence. At the same time, I also felt relief that I could honor my human feelings by not keeping them buried and repressed. There was a feeling of joy that this vivid childhood experience was symbolic of the trust I was trying to have in God, my Father. For the rest of that day, there was no question in my mind about feeling my father's presence within me, completely joined, completely at one. There was no separation between us.

Unbroken Communication

Finding peace in death through healed vision was also demonstrated to me by a woman in Washington, D.C. When she called me a few months ago, her husband was dying of cancer and didn't seem to have much longer to live. Although he had been in a coma for some time, she felt that he was continuing to suffer, and she was angry at God for letting this happen.

After I suggested that we share a few moments of joined silence, I felt guided to tell her that as long as she wanted to have everything under her control, including the time at which her husband was to die, she would be susceptible to anger and suffering. I told her that in one sense, she was trying to make her life *her* plan, rather than letting go and accepting God's plan for her life. I went on to say that as long as we are making judgments, we will be angry and unable to give unconditional love—something I knew she wanted to offer her husband.

I suggested that she forgive God and her misperceptions about Him, and that she let her will and His be one. I also suggested that she identify only with the light of love in her husband, and not with his body. I said that she could let her light of love, the essence of her being, simply join with the light of love in her husband.

She wrote me three weeks later, after her husband had died, telling me of the peace and joy she had experienced since we had last talked. She added that she still feels joined with her husband and is aware of his presence all the time. What freedom is given to all of us when we no longer have a need to control and judge! There is no loss through death when you view the world through the vision of love and trust in God.

I would also like to tell you about a mother who knew there was no death or separation. She wrote to me when her eighteen-year-old daughter, with whom I had worked, died of leukemia. In her letter, she stated that she replied to the many people who were offering her sympathy by saying, "If someone is lost, you don't know where she is. And I know where my daughter is; she and her love abide in the heart of God and right here in my heart all the time."

As these examples illustrate, it is possible to awaken from the sleep of our self-made illusions to the presence of God's love within us, and let go of thinking the body is our reality. Let us know that "communication is never broken, even when the body is destroyed, provided that we do not believe that bodies are essential for communication." Isn't that what Jesus taught the world by the resurrection?

Through healed vision I know there is no death.
The good news today is the same as it was over 2,000 years ago. With healed vision, we can know that there is no death, that life is never-ending, and that God's love and our relationship with Him is the only reality that there is.

Steps for Integrating Today's Lesson into Our Daily Life Experiences

1. Imagine a brilliant, glowing light around everyone you see or think of today. Know that the light you see is love and represents that person's true identity. Imagine the same brilliant light around yourself and see your light and the light of the other person joining as one. Know that the light you see

will never be extinguished as it is the reflection of eternal love, the creative force of the universe.

2. Close your eyes and think of someone you know who has died. Allow yourself to feel the loving presence of that person in the center of your heart. Recognize that you are joined to that person forever since love only joins and never dies.

3. Remind yourself that without fear and guilt you will recognize love as your only reality—and that through your healed vision there is no death. Repeat to yourself frequently throughout this day, "I am not a body; I am free. For I am still as God created me."*

4. At least once today read aloud the following poem, keeping in mind that your true identity is not a body but a nonphysical entity called love.

HEALING†

To heal it is not needful to allow
The thought of bodies to engulf your mind
In darkness and illusions. Healing is
Escape from all such thoughts. You hold instead
Only a single thought, which teaches you
Your brother is united with your mind,
So bodily intrusions on his peace
Cannot arise to jeopardize the Son
Whom God created sinless as Himself.
Think never of the body. Healing is
The thought of unity. Forget all things
That seem to separate. Your brother's pain
Has but one remedy; the same as yours.
He must be whole, because he joins with you
And you are healed, because you join with him.

*A Course in Miracles, Workbook, Lesson 199.
†From The Gifts of God, by Helen Schucman (The Foundation for Inner Peace, 1982), p. 27.

*"Peace is inevitable to those who
offer peace."*

Giving Love Away Is How I Keep It

We cannot really give peace and love to others until we accept them for ourselves. Peace and love begin from within, not from without. It is very easy for us to forget this principle, and when we do, we find ourselves in pain and conflict once again.

Love Renews Itself

When we are experiencing a lack of love in our lives, we frequently behave as though we are automobiles about to run out of gas. We search desperately for someone to fill us up with love in order to keep on going. We forget that love, which continually renews itself as we extend it to others, is the essence of our being. Instead, we perceive it as something outside ourselves, given to us by others in limited quantities, which we are constantly afraid will run out.

Search for Love

Many of us spend a great deal of time seeking love—believing that what we want and need is outside ourselves. We continue to place expectations on others to meet these needs and, sooner or later, we become disappointed and frustrated because we do not get what we think we want. Consequently, we often feel depressed, frustrated, and in conflict. We also feel justified anger, and our minds become filled with unforgiving, attack thoughts. When we are being love-seekers, the temptation to identify with our bodies becomes stronger than ever, and we act as though this distorted, limited concept of reality is a true reflection of who we are.

The reason we experience these limiting, negative thoughts and feelings is because we give our power away. When we give to others the option to decide for us whether we are going to be peaceful or in conflict, we reinforce the belief that we are victims of the world around us. Forgetting that we alone are responsible for our own peace, we conclude that whatever happens to us is caused by someone or something outside ourselves.

The Law of Abundance

There is another way of looking at the world, and that is to recognize that our true identity is spiritual—that our reality is love, and our body is simply a manifestation of form. It is to know that our spirit and minds are joined as one, and that we are not separate from one another.

As we are reminded in the 23d Psalm, our "cup runneth over"—the law of love is the law of abundance. What this means to me is that when we accept the truth that we remain as God created us, we can never experience lack because He has provided us with everything we need. It is also true that the only way we can experience love is to give it away, and, since the law of love *is* the law of abundance—the law of joining and of being joined—the more we give away, the more we have.

"Big Men" Do Cry

About six months after the movie *E.T.* came out, I had an opportunity—following a lecture I had given in Seattle—to attend a seven o'clock showing of that film in a local theater. I went alone and took an aisle seat next to a mother who was holding her four-year-old son in her lap.

The lights were still on, and while we were waiting for the movie to begin I said to the child, "Gee, you must have the softest seat in the whole theater!"

He smiled shyly and answered, "Yeah, I know." Then looking up at me he said, "You know, mister, I understand that a lot of people cry in this movie."

I said, "Well, yes, I've heard that, too."

Then he looked me up and down and said, "But you're a big man and big men don't cry, do they?"

I replied, "Well, I cry. I cry lots of times when I'm sad. Sometimes I even cry when I'm happy."

Shaking his head at me he said, "No, I don't believe that. Big men don't cry."

Then the lights went out and the movie started. About halfway through the movie, I felt someone tugging on my arm. I was aware of a little face peering into mine, and I heard a voice say, "Hey mister, you really are crying, aren't you?" Wiping a tear from his eye he said, "You know, I'm crying, too."

It occurred to me then how much our culture believes that grown men should behave differently from children or women in terms of joining and expressing love, and how this culturally imposed standard of behavior encourages separation. And for all of us it is the feeling of being separated, of being alone, that causes us the greatest distress. Experiencing oneness with this little boy, in an environment where we both felt equal and safe to share our laughter and our tears, was a precious gift to me. I felt immeasurably enriched that I was able to share my love with him and to receive his in return.

Flying Through Fear

Several years ago, in 1975, I was a passenger on an overnight flight from San Francisco to New York City, called, for obvious reasons, the "red-eye special." Since I had had a particularly heavy day of appointments and was feeling very tired, it felt good to sit back in my seat and relax—away from the telephone calls and the business of the day. About an hour and a half out of San Francisco, I heard the voice of a flight attendant announce, "We have a medical emergency. Is there a doctor on board?" Since I felt certain there must be a general practitioner or internist on the plane somewhere, I didn't answer the call.

A few minutes later the same voice, now quavering with nervousness, asked once again, "Is there a doctor on board?" This time I responded. As I left my seat and started down the aisle, I remember saying to myself in desperation, "God, please help me!" My anxiety arose from the knowledge that this was a medical emergency, and, as a psychiatrist who had not had any first-hand medical experience since my days as an intern, I did not feel qualified to handle this assignment. I knew I needed all the support I could get, and I can't begin to tell you how helpful it was for me to repeat those four words. As I continued to say them under my breath, I began to feel my fear subside.

I was directed toward the rear of the plane where I saw a middle-aged man surrounded by several crew members. He appeared to be unconscious. A quick check of his vital signs revealed a barely discernible pulse, which told me he was in serious difficulty, and I began to give him cardio-respiratory resuscitation immediately. Within a few moments his pulse returned, although it was quite weak and very irregular. He continued to drift in and out of consciousness. During an interval of wakefulness, I told him I was a physician and that we could help each other in this situation by feeling and visualizing the light of God's love surrounding us. I said that this light was a reminder that we are safe because God is always with us. He smiled and seemed reassured. I then began to administer oxygen while I checked his wallet for any information about him that might prove useful. My search disclosed a piece of paper indicating he had been released that day from a hospital where he had been treated for a heart attack and high blood pressure.

The captain of the plane had been watchfully waiting while this drama unfolded. When I gave him my evaluation of the man's condition, he offered to make an emergency landing if I felt that was necessary. I closed my eyes and, once again, asked for God's help. The answer I received was "yes." We made an emergency stopover at an airport in Arizona where we were met by an ambulance that took the patient to a local medical facility.

After obtaining the name of the hospital where he would be taken, I called from New York the following day to see how he was doing. He was able to speak with me directly and reported that his condition had improved greatly. The doctors did not think he would have to be hospitalized for more than a few days.

Within the next few weeks I received several letters from crew members and passengers on the flight commending me for the way I had handled this emergency. The writers of these letters also mentioned that I appeared to be very peaceful throughout this experience and that my peacefulness had enabled them to remain calm also.

I know that the peace and love they had experienced had come about because I had chosen to step aside and let God lead the way. I was not concerned about the outcome; my only goal was to follow the guidance I needed to help someone in distress. I also knew in my heart that if this incident had occurred six months earlier—before I had become a student of *A Course in Miracles*—I would have reacted very differently.

By giving love, I was able to accept it for myself. The peace that I had during this experience has validated for me that "giving love away is how I keep it." Rather than feeling unqualified to respond to this medical emergency, with God's help I was able to do what was needed. I continue to feel gratitude for this lesson in faith, and for the truth in the spiritual statement, "Ask and you will receive," which was so powerfully demonstrated to me during this experience.

Let us make a decision today to awaken to the presence of God's love within us, and to give that love away to everyone, excluding no one, as we practice today's lesson.

Giving love away is how I keep it. *I was mistaken in believing that I could give anyone anything other than what I want for myself. Since I want to experience peace, love, and forgiveness, these are the only gifts I would offer others. It is not charity on my part to offer forgiveness and love to others in place of attack. Rather, giving love away is the only way I can keep it for myself.*

Steps for Integrating Today's Lesson into Our Daily Life Experiences

1. Think of one person in your life whom you rely on and expect to meet your needs. Silently, say to this person: "I give you my love rather than the power to decide for me whether I am going to be peaceful or in conflict today." As you repeat this, recognize that you are already complete and whole within yourself, and that you no longer wish to hold on to the guilt that comes from believing that you are separate and dependent on another.

2. Say to each person you encounter or even think of today: "Peace, love, and forgiveness are the only gifts I want, and so these are the gifts I offer you."

3. As each hour passes today, decide that this is the time for extending peace instead of conflict.

4. If you are feeling depressed, fearful, or guilty today, select someone—anyone will do—and for just one second concentrate on loving that person totally and completely. You don't have to say a word, and the person doesn't have to be in your physical environment. Just focus on giving your love to that person, and you will feel the healing power of love in your own life.

5. Learn today that giving and receiving are the same by saying in every situation or interaction you experience throughout the day: "Giving love away is how I keep it for myself. Am I now giving what I want to keep?"

*"Release from guilt as you would
be released."*

LESSON EIGHT

Forgiveness Releases Me from My Past

If our lives are not going well, or we are feeling a lack of love, we are often tempted to look for some person or situation in our external environment to blame. Forgiveness is letting go of whatever we think people, the world, or God has done to us as well as whatever we think we have done to them. As mentioned previously, it is through "celestial amnesia," that is, selective memory, that we can release all of our past memories and experiences except for the love we have given and received. It is through forgiveness that our misperceptions can be corrected.

There is a beautiful description of forgiveness from *A Course in Miracles* which has helped me so many times in my own struggle to release the past that I would like to share it with you.

Forgiveness paints a picture of a world where suffering is over, loss becomes impossible and anger makes no sense. Attack is gone, and madness has an end. What suffering is now conceivable? What loss can be sustained? The world becomes a place of joy, abundance, charity, and endless giving. It is now so like to Heaven that it quickly is transformed into the light that it reflects. And so the journey which the Son of God began has ended in the light from which he came.*

Principles for Peace

In order to practice forgiveness as our single function, it is essential to train ourselves to concentrate on peace of mind as our single goal. To help me remember this, I made up what I call "the three cardinal principles for experiencing peace:"

HAVE PEACE OF MIND, PEACE OF GOD, AS MY SINGLE GOAL.

HAVE FORGIVENESS AS MY ONLY FUNCTION.

POSTPONE MAKING ANY DECISIONS UNTIL I HAVE QUIETED MY MIND AND LISTENED TO MY INNER VOICE. (Other names for "inner voice" are voice of God, inner teacher, gut feeling, intuition.)

Blocks to the Awareness of Peace

I am convinced that children are our greatest teachers of forgiveness since they seem to be able to practice it so

---

**A Course in Miracles*, Workbook, Lesson 249.

much more easily than we adults. Think how many times you have heard your child or someone else's say to a playmate in a fit of anger, "I'm never going to play with you again!" Yet what seems like only moments later, you look up and see them happily involved in a game, laughing together as though nothing had happened. We adults, however, seem to feel justified in carrying grudges and holding on to grievances for months—even years. We forget that all attack thoughts begin in our own mind. When we are being unforgiving to others, it is actually ourselves we are unable to forgive.

The goal of our ego is conflict, anger, murder, and war. Peace of mind is the enemy of our ego. Our ego attempts to achieve its goal by continually evaluating our own behavior or judging the reactions of others to determine who is guilty. Like a robot, our ego continues to recycle guilt while it judges, condemns, and punishes.

As long as we believe that our physical perceptions define what is real, we will be tempted to evaluate and make condemning judgments. And the moment we make a condemning judgment, our peace of mind is gone and the presence of God disappears.

Forgiveness—the Ultimate Challenge

Recently I had an experience that offered my ego a field day. I found myself tempted to make a string of interpretations and condemning judgments regarding the various people I heard about in a very tragic, true life story. This is what happened.

I received a phone call from a woman who said she was on a spiritual pathway and was studying *A Course in Miracles*. She said that intellectually she knew that God's love was her only reality and everything else was an illusion, but that everything around her right now, including her own sense of guilt, seemed quite real.

She went on to tell me that for the last year, there had been a number of articles in newspapers throughout the country about a two-and-one-half-year-old girl who had been kidnapped and held captive in a van for ten months by an adult male and a teenage boy. During this time, the girl was repeatedly subjected to sexual abuse. Both the man and his teenage accomplice were finally apprehended, and, after a lengthy trial, the man was sentenced to prison for over 500 years with no chance of parole.

The woman stated that her name was Mrs. Cabarga and that the teenage boy, who was a juvenile when the crime was committed, was her son, Alex. She added that Alex would be appearing before the judge for sentencing in a few weeks, and she wanted to know if I could help her find inner peace. I really didn't know what I could say that would be helpful, but I invited her to come to my office the next day. My inner guidance was to have female energy present during our meeting, and, after checking this out with Mrs. Cabarga, I invited my dear friend and spiritual partner, Diane Cirincione, to participate in the interview.

This is the story that Mrs. Cabarga told us. In an attempt to resolve difficulties within the family, she and her husband decided to become involved a number of years ago in a communal living experiment in a San Francisco warehouse. Her son, Alex, the youngest of five children, was nine years old at the time. When the family's domestic problems were not resolved in this new environment, Mrs. Cabarga became emotionally distraught and confused. With the encouragement of her husband and children, she made a decision to leave the commune and live independently. She and her husband agreed that Alex could stay with "Tree Frog," a man in the commune who seemed to be very fond of children and had taken a special interest in their son.

Later, she and her husband reunited and began to see their son on a monthly basis. When Alex reached his eighteenth birthday, Mrs. Cabarga and her husband decided to give him a party. However, he failed to show up for the celebration. The next day the newspapers came out revealing that Alex and his "guardian," the man called Tree Frog, had been arrested and were being held on kidnapping and sexual abuse charges.

Mrs. Cabarga's feelings of guilt and self-blame were overwhelming. She convinced herself that she was one of the most irresponsible, unloving, and selfish women in the world. And the widespread media publicity only reinforced her negative self-image.

As the story unfolded, it was revealed that her son had been consistently beaten, sexually abused, and mistreated for the nine years that he had lived with Tree Frog. Mrs. Cabarga told us that the court-appointed psychiatrist, as well as many others who knew the details of the case, felt Alex was a victim who needed treatment. However, there was so much public outrage that it looked as though her son would not be placed in a rehabilitation program for adolescents, but rather would be subject to sentencing as an adult criminal and sent away to prison for the rest of his life.

On the human level, I think it is most difficult to have equal compassion for all those involved in this horrifying scenario. One's heart wants to be fully open to the tragic circumstances surrounding the little girl and her parents. And one's mind is tempted to feel justifiable anger toward the two who were apprehended. In the ego's judgment, some things that happen are considered unforgivable.

Yet, I am convinced that unless our hearts and minds are open to extend equal compassion to all, complete forgiveness and love to all, we will not experience inner peace. And, therefore, we will not be able to give our peace to others; we will simply contribute to the continuation of conflict in the world. At the same time, we must also remember that forgiveness does not mean condoning the acts that have been described in this situation.

As we were interviewing Mrs. Cabarga, I was aware that the following hour I would be leading the co-learning session at The Center for Attitudinal Healing. During this weekly public meeting, principles of attitudinal healing are discussed in some detail. Diane and I decided to invite Mrs. Cabarga to attend the meeting with us in the hope that it might give her an opportunity to experience something that perhaps had not been available to her before—unconditional love, acceptance, and forgiveness. This co-learning session was an especially powerful one that allowed all of us, including Mrs. Cabarga, to look at our temptations to judge others rather than to offer them forgiveness.

The following week, Mrs. Cabarga asked Diane and me if we would visit Alex in jail. After obtaining a court order, we went to see him. During his many months in jail, he had engaged in much introspection and had accepted responsibility for his actions. Alex was in the process of turning to God for help and also eager to help others in any way he could.

Before leaving the jail I asked him, on the basis of what he had been learning about himself, what advice he might like to give others. Alex replied, "Don't be afraid to look at yourself. Don't be afraid to find things out about yourself, because it is only then that you will be able to begin to do something about them and free yourself. Otherwise, your mind will remain in prison and that's much worse than the bars that imprison me."

Alex also stated that he had been thinking about the subject of forgiveness a lot. He had experienced tremendous anger and hate for Tree Frog as the facts of his brainwashing unfolded at the trial. However, he knew deep in his heart that he would never experience true inner peace until he could completely forgive his abuser. Although it is not easy for him, he commented that each day he tries to hold Tree Frog "in the light."

Alex Cabarga was recently sentenced to 208 years in prison.

The media have made all of us aware of the increasing incidents of sexual abuse today, and the damage experienced by all parties involved. In one sense, the problem can be looked upon as one of spiritual deprivation—a feeling of being separate from the love of God and each other. It is as though some aspect underlying our American culture is screaming out, "Help! I feel alone; I have no love in my life. I want love, I am afraid of love, I am confused. Help me find love!"

I don't believe that our society, or the world, can be healed until we learn to forgive everyone and to exclude no one from our love. To me, there is no more important concept than the healing power of forgiveness, because forgiveness brings us the release we need in order to see ourselves and the world differently. Let us continue to retrain our minds and keep in our hearts and consciousness the following thoughts:

Forgiveness releases me from my past. *Whenever I see someone else as guilty, I am reinforcing my own sense of guilt and unworthiness. I cannot forgive myself unless I am willing to forgive others. It does not matter what I think anyone has done to me in the past or what I think I may have done. Only through forgiveness can my release from guilt and fear be complete.*

Steps for Integrating Today's Lesson into Our Daily Life Experiences

1. If you find yourself blaming someone today, stop and reflect on the following. If you had gone through the same childhood and life experiences as the person you are judging against, isn't it possible

that you might behave in a similar manner? Then see the scared and fearful child in that person who, if he or she felt perfect love, would not be behaving that way. Forgive and send them love.

2. Review at least twice during the day the "three cardinal principles for experiencing peace":

I am determined to have peace of mind, peace of God, as my single goal today.

I am determined to have forgiveness as my only function today.

I will postpone making any decisions today until I have quieted my mind and listened to my inner voice.

3. If you feel tempted today—regardless of the seeming justification—to blame anyone, remind yourself that in the loving eyes of God we are all sinless and innocent.

4. Choose today to let go of all your past misperceptions about yourself and others. Instead, be determined to join with everyone you meet or even think about today and say, "I see you and myself only in the light of true forgiveness."

5. Accept the happiness and joy that you have earned today through your practice of complete and total forgiveness of yourself and others.

*"With love in you, you have no
need except to extend it."*

LESSON NINE

I Can Know Love
Only in the Present

Love can only be experienced in the present, and it is only through love that we can reach beyond time to timelessness. Although most of us have great difficulty living in the present moment, infants, who have not yet adapted to the concept of linear time with a past, present, and future, seem to be able to do this quite easily. They relate only in the immediate present, and, consequently, it is my belief that, unlike us adults, they do not experience a world based on fragmentation and separation.

A newborn child is a beautiful symbol of unconditional love. Infants are not concerned with their parents' past or future, what they look like or how they talk, or even whether or not they are worthy of love. The infant symbolizes knowledge not as an accumulation of fragmented facts, but as love, which is true knowledge. Love is the essence of the newborn's being, and the light that an infant reflects can only be a reflection of God's love. With willingness to trust and live each moment to the fullest, a newborn child teaches us that each instant can be a new opportunity for extending and expanding love.

The Ego's Use of Time

Our ego-mind, however, uses time for a very different purpose. Its purpose is to judge, to attack, and to separate. As we discussed earlier, our ego would have us believe that our reality is based on the input our brain receives from the physical senses. This input is interpreted in terms of the past, present, and future. In this way, linear time becomes a necessary illusion for the ego's survival.

This belief system, to which most of us still subscribe, encourages us to project our past learning onto the future, insuring that our future will be like the past. Thus, in satisfying our need to control and predict, we all but eliminate the possibility of experiencing love and happiness in the present moment. Contrast this fear-based projection with the way a newborn child, who has no need to control the future, relates to life by concentrating full attention on living completely in the present moment.

A Course in Miracles suggests that the true purpose of time is to recognize that "God's will for us is perfect happiness," right now.

God's Presence

God's presence can only be experienced in the present instant. The moment we dwell upon experiences from our past or become preoccupied with the future, we let the ego block our ability to experience God's love in the present. To awaken to the possibility of the reality of love—in which worry and anxiety are totally absent—we must first be willing to let go of our attachment to the past and anticipation of the future. Then we can recognize that our unchanging state is one of love, joy, and peace.

It is possible for all of us to focus on the peace of God as our only goal and forgiveness as our only function for just one instant. In that instant we can give up judging and evaluating, and trust that the voice of love will direct and guide us. If we are willing to do this for just one moment, our future can become an extension of a peaceful and loving present that never ceases.

Messenger of Truth

In practicing today's lesson, I have found the following process helpful. Imagine that the entire universe is made up only of light and that you are at the center of that light—in the heart of God. Recognize that your only reality is light. Now, while staying in the consciousness of that light, step into the world of illusion on the planet earth. Imagine that during that one second you are on earth, all you have to do is let your light shine on and through all minds. Then step back into the center of light once again. For that one, brief instant, while you were in the world of illusion, know that you were a messenger of God—a messenger of truth—bringing love and light to a world filled with fear and darkness.

As a messenger of love, we don't have to judge or evaluate; we don't have to do anything except let the Christ light, which has always been in us, shine through. It naturally shines on everything and excludes nothing. As we repeat this process, reminding ourselves each time that "I can know love only in the present," our minds will experience the joy that comes from bringing light to a world of darkness. In this way, we awaken to the knowledge that we have never really left the heart of God, which is our home.

Celebration of Love

I would like to tell you about a project at The Redwoods, a retirement home in Mill Valley, California. This project was started a couple of years ago by Mary Cole, a wonderful eighty-seven-year-old woman who lives there. Mary had read about our work at The Center for Attitudinal Healing and felt that the principles we use could be very helpful to herself and other elderly people.

Mary's premise was that most people in retirement homes spend a lot of time living in the past and being very fearful about the future. They often have numerous complaints and grudges—many of which center on the infrequency of visits from family members or friends. They are likely to be preoccupied with physical complaints and the temptation to feel sorry for themselves is great. Their feelings of helplessness and loneliness contribute to an outlook on life that is frequently despairing and hopeless.

Mary asked us to assist her in introducing a program in attitudinal healing at The Redwoods to help these elderly people find another way of looking at the world. We were delighted to accept her invitation and have been supporting and collaborating with her on this project ever since. The program consists of weekly group discussions that include material on attitudinal healing. Mary and one or two representatives from the center facilitate these groups, and sometimes I participate in these sessions as well.

The purpose of these meetings is to enable the residents to apply the principles of attitudinal healing in their daily lives. It has been a wonderful blessing for me to witness this process. Seeing perceptions changing and people developing a feeling of dignity and usefulness as they help each other reconfirms our belief that continued personal growth is possible at any age. The conditions of growth center on trust and faith in God, unconditional love, forgiveness, and living with joy in the present instant.

Last fall my schedule became unusually busy, and I was not able to visit The Redwoods for several months. However, my workload lightened up in January, and I again made plans to visit The Redwoods. En route to the meeting I passed a flower stand, and it occurred to me that it would be great fun to present a flower to each member of the group; so I bought three dozen roses.

I was completely unprepared for the extent of gratitude expressed for this small remembrance! I discovered that it had been years since many of these people had received flowers. On a subsequent visit, I learned that several members of the group put their roses in the refrigerator at night to preserve their freshness so they could enjoy them longer. I was overwhelmed at how this simple gift could bring such joy—not only to them, but to myself. This experience brought to life for me the principle of attitudinal healing that "giving and receiving are one in truth."

A few weeks later, I received the following guidance during a morning meditation: to have children make individual presentations of a rose—accompanied by a hug—to each of the three hundred residents at The Redwoods on Valentine's Day. I discussed this project with Mary and the center's staff, and their enthusiasm was immediate. We began to make plans to carry out our Valentine's Day surprise.

First we made arrangements for children from the center, as well as children of staff members and friends, to participate in the project. Then a volunteer from the center went to the San Francisco flower mart to see if we could get the roses wholesale, but the answer was no since roses are in great demand at that time of the year. A few days later a friend of mine, hearing about our project, put me in touch with a flower-grower who supplies the wholesale market. When I telephoned him with our request he immediately offered to give us the flowers free. He said, "After all, money isn't everything. It is helping others that really counts—and this giving is not only going to make them happy, it's going to make my Valentine's Day the best I've ever had!"

Next we needed three hundred individual containers to put the roses in. Bud vases were too expensive for us to buy, and it occurred to me that empty Perrier bottles might solve our problem. The local bars in Tiburon were very cooperative in this regard and agreed to save them for us. It soon became clear, however, that we would not have a sufficient supply in time for Valentine's Day. At this point someone suggested that we call the Calistoga Sparkling Mineral Water Bottling Company in a nearby town to see if the company could help us out with containers. When we explained our project to them, they agreed to send us, free, all the empty Calistoga bottles that we needed. I arrived at the retirement center late in the morning on Valentine's Day to find 350 unopened Calistoga bottles filled with sparkling mineral water! At first it seemed like we had another problem on our hands. There was not enough time to empty the bottles, and we wondered if the soda water would kill the roses. However, we all learned something new from that experience. What we found out was that the roses actually live longer in sparkling water than in regular water!

As our Valentine's Day surprise got underway, the children went down the halls knocking on each resident's door. When it was opened, they introduced themselves and presented the roses—giving each elderly person a warm hug along with the flower. I saw smiles of appreciation appear on the faces of many people who I bet hadn't smiled that way in years. Tears of joy shone in the eyes of the residents and were reflected in our own eyes as well, as we witnessed this moving scene unfold many times that day.

During that one moment of giving—when the love and hugs were going both ways—none of us was thinking of the past. There was no holding on to grudges. There was only joining. There was only the celebration of life, the celebration of love. In the nowness of that moment, there was only joy.

The experience of that day at The Redwoods remains very deep in my heart. Every time I recall it, these are the thoughts which occur to me: how simple it is to give; how much easier it is to share joy rather than complain; how much easier it is to love than to hate; how much easier it is to live in the moment of now rather than in the past or future.

I can know love only in the present. *My preoccupation with the past and its projection into the future defeats my aim of present peace. Peace cannot be found in the past or future, but only now, in this instant. The past is over and the future is yet to be.*

Steps for Integrating Today's Lesson into Our Daily Life Experiences

1. Write down three ways you can give your love to others today without expecting anything in return. Select one of these ways and actually commit yourself to sharing your love with someone today.

2. For just one instant today, focus on accepting the peace of God as your only goal. Remind yourself that God is *never* in the past or future, but only in the present. You can accept His peace *now*.

3. At least twice today practice the following "messenger of truth" process described in today's lesson:

Imagine that the entire universe is made up only of light and that you are at the center of that light—in the heart of God. Recognize that your only reality is light. Now, while staying in the consciousness of that light, step into the world of illusion on the planet earth. Imagine that during that one second you are on earth, all you have to do is let your light shine on and through all minds. Then step back into the center of light once again. For that one, brief instant, while you were in the world of illusion, know that you were a messenger of God—a messenger of truth—bringing love and light to a world filled with fear and darkness.

Remember that as a messenger of truth you don't have to judge or evaluate, you don't have to do anything, except let the Christ-light shine through.

4. For just one moment let everything else go from your mind. Now—in this instant— accept the joy that is your natural inheritance as a bringer of light to others.

*"All healing is release from
the past."*

LESSON TEN

Without the Past I Claim My Freedom Now

I s it possible that this world and everything in it are only a dream? Is it possible that our mind has split itself off from God, our only Source, and deluded us into believing that we live in a world where separation, pain, and death are real? Is it possible that we are simply asleep and do not know it?

It is my belief that as we awaken to the truth that love is what we really are, we begin to realize that we have spent aeons reenacting old scripts that our minds have made up. It is our ego-mind that has written, produced, and played all the roles in these dramatic productions, whose primary purpose is to project the illusion that we are separate from each other.

Personal Soap Operas

As we begin to wake up, we recognize how strongly attached we have been to these old dramas—which are really our personal soap operas—even though they all have the same repetitious theme. Whether explicitly stated or cleverly disguised, the unvarying message is that we live in a world where separation is a reality. Opposing forces can never be reconciled, punishment and despair are inevitable, the past predicts the future, and lasting joy and peace are impossible. In our unawakened state, the endless variations on this theme appear to be quite normal and realistic. In truth, they depict an insane, unreal world in which trust and faith are viewed as short-lived flights into fantasy, and unconditional love is nonexistent.

When I was a teenager in Long Beach, California, I had a job ushering in a theater. I once remember watching a John Wayne movie for so many months that I actually began to walk and talk like him— although I am quick to add that I never looked like him! I realize now that working in that theater was symbolically important for me. Although I wasn't aware of it then, I have since come to know that everything we experience in our lives is really an outward projection of our own inner psychological state of mind. In the process of externalizing our psychological state, we come to believe that the world we see is outside ourselves. What we fail to recognize, however, is that this "outside" world is really only the reflection of our own thoughts and fantasies. As long as we continue to relive these old soap operas from our past, our awakening to truth will be delayed. For as *A Course in Miracles* tells us, unless the past is over in our mind, the real world must escape our sight.

Release from the Past

How, then, can we see the world as it truly is and awaken to the reality of love's presence in our lives—the world that forgiveness offers us? We can do this only by being willing to release ourselves and others from all the errors of the past. Great spiritual teachers have taught us that it is possible to forgive everyone—even those who we feel have hurt us most. As children of God we, too, have been empowered to transcend our illusions by choosing to see the world through love's eyes—the eyes of forgiveness.

All of us have hurtful memories from our past. In order to protect ourselves from repeating these painful experiences in the future, we build up our defenses. In using our fearful past to predict a fearful future, we are unable to live without fear in the present.

Since we cannot experience fear and love simultaneously, we must recognize that the past is over and can no longer affect us. We can live in the present, and in the presence of love, only by releasing the past through forgiveness.

The "Holiest of Spots"

As an illustration of today's lesson, I would like to share with you an experience I had about two years ago. My coauthor, Dr. William Thetford (who, along with Dr. Helen Schucman, was responsible for bringing *A Course in Miracles* into being), and I had accepted an invitation to consult with the medical staff at Travis Air Force Base in California to discuss how principles from the course, that is, attitudinal healing principles, could be applied to the medical model. This turned out to be the first of many such consultations that have continued to the present day.

During the hour and a half drive from Tiburon to Travis,

I felt a growing anxiety about how I would react once we arrived at the base. The reason for all this inner turmoil was that during the Korean War years from 1953 to 1954, I had been stationed at Travis as a staff psychiatrist, and those two years proved to be very difficult ones for me. I resented military life. I hated having to wear a uniform. In short, I could hardly wait until I would become a civilian again. On the day when I received my discharge from Travis, I remember selling the uniform right off my back and announcing in a loud voice, "Thank God I will never have to set foot on this base again!" And here I was, almost thirty years later, driving back to that very base to talk about—of all things—the power of forgiveness!

Unfortunately, I had not done my homework as far as forgiving the armed services was concerned. In that regard I was still very much stuck in the past. In my mind I continued to think that attack and defense were the only interests of the military, and I had great difficulty believing that a talk on love and forgiveness would be enthusiastically received at an air force base. My fearful past was clearly encouraging me to predict a fearful future, and the military provided a very convenient "screen" for the projection of my own attack thoughts.

At Bill's suggestion we stopped to meditate for a few minutes before arriving at the base. As we prayed together, I chose to see all the experiences I had perceived as negative during my two years at Travis as illusions, and I reminded myself that illusions have no value. I knew that all I needed was a little willingness to ask the Holy Spirit to help me let go of the past. And my request did not go unanswered. By the time we arrived, I felt at peace. At the end of our consultation I was grateful that I had been given an opportunity to share my thoughts about the healing power of love and forgiveness with the medical staff there. If I had not been willing to recognize that the past was truly over, I could not have shared in the miracle of love that occurred that afternoon.

I continue to be at peace each time I go to the base to

consult, and I smile as I remember the concept from *A Course in Miracles* that states: "The holiest of all the spots on earth is where an ancient hatred has become a present love."

Awakening to the Reality of Love

I would like to share with you a letter that, to me, demonstrates how once we truly say, "Without the past I claim my freedom now," the world we see becomes different.

Jerry:

It's difficult to describe in words the depth of experience that has transformed me recently. I had begun to think that I was incapable of experiencing love, that I was a victim of events and people around me.

I discovered at an early age that I was gay, and at that age it was a nonissue. It seemed so natural. Slowly I built up a defense system, walls and barriers to protect myself from being vulnerable. I didn't realize that through denying myself true expression and recognition of myself, I wasn't allowing myself to experience other areas of my being.

I had never been involved in a "relationship" (I'm twenty-five) until last year, when a very loving and caring man came into my life. He poured much love into me, and I felt his need for my love, but refused to accept that I wanted or needed his or anybody's love.

I could see in his eyes his truth and giving, and it wasn't until we split up that I felt that it was real. I was going away for a two-week vacation and stopped in to a bookstore downtown to see if

I could begin to expose myself to new ideas. I kept telling myself that there must be another way of experiencing life. Some mornings I would awake with dread at the day facing me. Work was a chore for the most part.

I saw *Love Is Letting Go of Fear,* and the title intrigued me because those two words, *Love* and *Fear,* were the words that this man had said to me. He had told me I was too afraid to love.

I read your book on my vacation and forgot all about the pressures and priorities of my business. It said something to me, and I started to apply some of the ideas to my own life.

It wasn't until I returned that I reread the book—twice—slowly and deliberately listening to every line. I kept the ideas in your book a priority for three days and began to feel an amazing transformation. I was experiencing things differently because I *chose* to. I was feeling the seed of human potential for the first time in my life.

On the third day I had an amazing day. I seemed to feel energy pressing through every inch of my body. I was so charged by life and interaction with people that I felt I couldn't touch enough.

That night I came home and couldn't stop smiling. . . . I fell asleep and woke up about an hour later. Suddenly I felt the warmth of the previous day stirring in my body, and an intense wave of vibration passed over me from head to toe. It was so intense that I felt I was losing control because the tears were rolling down my cheeks. In my mind I kept telling myself not to fear this experience. Then, from below my navel, I felt an even more intense stirring warmth and SAW a light being generated from my abdomen. I was in a state of suspension and kept wondering if I was dreaming, but it was REAL.

I felt I wanted to hug every person in my life. All aspects of each person's warmth and radiance were filling every cell of my being! Faces and smiles were flashing before my eyes.

I cried and cried at the sheer joy and intensity of LIFE. I looked at the clock when the wave and vibration had subsided. For two hours I had been in a state of ecstasy!

The next morning I arose and couldn't get the day started fast enough. I had a million things to do, and each was teaching me something. The more I felt and generated love, the less room there was for fear. The work seemed so wonderful, and every person I came in contact with I wanted to touch, to stir, to experience.

The sheer joy of living was so intense! I felt as though I didn't have to eat or sleep! Over the following week, the intensity subsided; but I am, quite simply, a new person now.

I am *feeling* life and it feels so good. I just want to keep growing in all areas. I love my family and friends so much. . . . And it's coming so naturally. I broke down walls, which were years in the building, when I released through my tears.

I feel strong. I'm glad to be alive. I'm so happy you shared your ideas with the world, because they are so universal. They go beyond the doctrine and dogma of a religion, yet contain the elements of so many.

Be well. I hope someday I can hear you speak; but, if not, I feel your life through your words and experience we *are* all one.

Love,
(signed)*George*

Without the past I claim my freedom now. *Only if I keep reliving the past in the present am I a slave to time. By forgiving and letting go of the past, I free my-*

self of the painful burdens I have carried into the present. Now, I can claim the opportunities for freedom in the present without my past distortions.

Today, freedom is my goal as I say: I choose to claim my release from past pain and suffering by living only in the immediate present.

Steps for Integrating Today's Lesson into Our Daily Life Experiences

1. Identify for yourself one old script in your personal soap opera that you continue to replay on your internal TV set. Decide today to release yourself from the limitations of this script by saying: "As a child of God, I can let go my painful past and choose to see the world through the eyes of love—the eyes of forgiveness."

2. Visualize all the hurtful memories from your past extending behind you on a long strip of carpet. Now see yourself roll up the carpet and dispose of it. Allow yourself to experience the past as truly gone and enjoy the opportunity for happiness in the present moment.

3. At least once today, devote five minutes to meditating on the concept of today's lesson: *Without the past I claim my freedom now.*

4. Identify any difficulties you may be having in a past or present relationship. Now ask yourself the question, "What grievance am I holding on to that is limiting my freedom?" Remember that forgiveness can be instantaneous and decide today to let go of all grievances—past or present—and claim your freedom now.

"To love yourself is to heal yourself."

LESSON ELEVEN

Only My
Condemnation
Injures Me*

I never fail to be impressed with how frequently my mind can become split—how often my ego can interfere with my peace by condemning me or choosing to attack someone else. Indeed, it is important not to underestimate our ego's potential for disturbing our peace even when we feel that our minds are focused and conflict-free.

Peace Threatens the Ego

When we are experiencing peace of mind, our ego is likely to feel threatened and want to get rid of that peace immediately. Since the ego is confused about pain and happiness, it makes guilt seem attractive to us. It wants us

*A Course in Miracles, Title of Workbook Lesson 198.

to believe that our body is our true reality, and that death is really the end of life.

The power of the ego-mind to disrupt our lives when we least expect it became very clear to me one day last year when I was in Hawaii on a lecture tour. Since I like to start my day with exercise whenever possible, I had gotten up early one morning to go for a run. It was a beautiful day, and I jogged along repeating to myself favorite quotations from *A Course in Miracles*. As I continued to run, I found myself feeling especially peaceful and at one with God.

I had not gone very far, however, when I suddenly spotted a beer can lying conspicuously in the middle of a well-manicured golf course I had been admiring along my route. Immediately I made a judgment about the unknown person who had deposited the can there, spoiling the natural beauty of the green. The moment I made that judgment, I noticed that my peacefulness began to disappear.

All of a sudden I began to recall the times in my own life when I had thoughtlessly tossed things out of my car window. I realized that I still felt guilty about those past actions and that I needed to release these feelings. By this time, my ego-mind had turned my peaceful run into a guilt trip, and I decided to ask the Holy Spirit to help me let go of my self-condemnation and guilt.

My inner teacher responded by telling me that if I really wanted to release myself from the past and experience peace, I needed to return to the golf course and remove the unsightly can. "But it's at least a mile or so back there," I began to argue with myself. Then as I recognized the meddlesome voice of my ego once again, I turned myself around and ran back to complete my assignment. The instant I picked up the can I felt a sense of joy and peace. I knew I had done the right thing. It gave me great pleasure to see the natural beauty of the green no longer flawed by the ill-placed can and to know I had played a small part in enabling others to enjoy that beauty also.

The Litter of Self-Condemnation

As I look back on my own life, I now realize that my mind was preoccupied with the litter of self-condemnation and the condemnation of others. I condemned myself for being clumsy, hyperactive, and shy, for being a poor student, and—although it seems ridiculous now—for not being able to sing in tune. In general, I thought of myself as a slob. I felt I would never do anything right, that others would dislike me, and I even resented my Jewish background. I remember at one time condemning my parents for being Jewish—because if it weren't for that, I would be like everyone else and not subject to anti-Semitic attacks. What an enormous release it has been for me to learn more and more how to detach myself from the past and let go of my guilt and condemnation. What a joy it is to feel the weight of the world lift off my shoulders as I am increasingly able to practice forgiveness, accept myself, and experience God's presence in my life.

The Mirror of Love

When we condemn ourselves or others, we are allowing our minds to be fed by fearful illusions created by our ego, and we become imprisoned by these distortions. We need to remind ourselves constantly that love is the only reality there is, and anything we perceive that does not mirror love is a misperception, an illusion. And the only way we can correct these misperceptions is to forgive ourselves and others by letting go of whatever we think we may have done to them or they to us.

Since our true reality is but an extension and expansion

of God's love—a thought in the mind of God—when we adhere to His laws, there is no separation, time, or space. However, our ego does not want us to believe that a loving God exists, and that our reality is simply an expression of His love. Rather, it tries to convince us that our true reality is our physical form—our body. It is a misperception to think that any form that changes can be real. Indeed, it is very hard for us to accept the idea that this material world and the bodies in it are simply illusions.

The Split-Mind Trap

Since the ego-mind finds truth extremely threatening, it works very hard to persuade us that our illusions are real. We cannot believe in the world of illusion and in the reality of God's love at the same time without experiencing conflict and split-mindedness. I am convinced, however, that as long as we are on this earth, we will always be tempted to act as though the physical world and everything in it is real.

Whenever I am tempted to believe that one illusion may be more valid or desirable than another, I try to remember that all illusions add up to 0, and therefore $0 + 0$ always equals 0. And yet, as *A Course in Miracles* tells us "illusion makes illusion," and as long as we believe we can injure or condemn others, we, in turn, must feel others can harm us. In reality, however, it is impossible to condemn ourselves or others because we can only hurt or be hurt when we think that we are separate from our Source.

"Don't Bite the Apple"

The following story is about a friend of mine, Linda Berdeski, who was able to stop condemning and punishing herself when she made the crucial decision to join with the love from which she had never really been separated.

Less than ten years ago, Linda, a divorced mother of four children, "bottomed out." She wound up on skid row, broke, and addicted to alcohol and drugs. Her sense of self-esteem was about as low as it could get, and her self-condemnation was at an all-time high.

One day while sitting at a bar in San Diego, Linda came to the sudden realization that she had a choice. She recognized that either she could continue to drink herself into oblivion, or she could take responsibility for herself and turn her life around. Within moments she had made her decision. She told her drinking companions that she was no longer willing to live the life of an alcoholic, and, having made that statement, she left her past life behind her as she walked out of the darkened bar into the bright noonday sun.

Linda told me that as she stepped into the sunlight she felt the growing warmth of God's presence surrounding her and supporting her decision. In the next few weeks, she sought the help she needed to break herself of her addictions and begin a new life. She let go of her attachments to the painful and fearful past, as well as her anxieties about the possibility of a troubled future. In short, she put herself in the hands of God. As she began to practice forgiveness of everyone, including herself, she began to see the positive effects in her life that came from placing her trust in God.

Shortly after Linda stopped drinking, she began volunteering at a center for alcoholics. Several months later, a job opening for a counselor came up at the center, and she applied for it. Although Linda had no college education or professional counseling experience—and a number of other applicants were highly qualified—she got the position.

I asked her why she felt she was the one to be chosen despite her lack of credentials, and her answer really intrigued me. She replied, "When they asked me why I thought I would be good for the job, something came out of my mouth that absolutely amazed me. I heard myself saying, 'I want to help people and I'm probably the most magnificent person you'll ever meet in your life!' Believe me, in my wildest thoughts I could never have imagined myself saying anything like that; it was almost as though someone else spoke those words for me. And the next thing I knew, I had the job!"

For the following two and a half years, Linda taught positive thinking at the center, and her own life changed in miraculous ways. "The theories of Christ work if you use them," Linda says. "In the Bible, Christ says to Simon Peter, 'Do you love me?' And Simon Peter replies, 'Lord, you know that I love you.' Then Christ responds, 'Feed my sheep.'" And in Linda's words, "The way we do that is to feed—mentally and physically—the people who need it."

Four years ago in response to the need of the homeless and hungry of Imperial Beach, California—a suburb of San Diego near the Mexican border—Linda opened a tiny restaurant called My Little Cafe. Linda describes her restaurant, which is located in the midst of an economically depressed area along the waterfront, as a "kind of masquerade—it is a front for God." And, as anyone who has ever been there can tell you, that is exactly what it is.

Each day, in addition to serving breakfast, lunch, and dinner in her cafe to those who can pay the modest cost of a meal, Linda and her volunteers, which often included her teenage children, bring soup and sandwiches to the pier right outside their door. They feed homeless alcoholics, drug addicts, runaway youths, or anyone else who is hungry but unable to afford the price of a meal. "We feed them whatever is available to us," she says. Nor is her "feeding" limited to supplying food. Individuals who come to the cafe for help are provided with emergency aid such as temporary housing and clothing, as well as books or transportation to the alcoholic detoxification center in San Diego where she once worked.

The idea for the cafe has led Linda to other related activities. In fact, My Little Cafe is the center of an entire organization including a church with the unusual name, "Don't Bite the Apple." Linda has explained the meaning of this name in her own eloquent way:

> You and I are continually playing the parts of Adam and Eve in the Garden. Every time we judge another, we are biting the apple of condemnation. Every time we influence another person to criticize or condemn, we are tempting Adam. Every time we let human judgment of good and evil govern our thinking, we are cast out of Paradise.

> The formula for staying in Paradise is simple. Practice, practice, practice not biting the apple. You will find as you practice that you will try to stay in a constant state of giving to others. You will begin to find yourself in a natural state of unconditional love and extend it to others. We, ourselves, make the choice whether to live in or out of the blissful state of Paradise. It is a conscious choice.

Linda is also a devoted student of *A Course in Miracles* and teaches regular evening classes on the application of the course's principles to everyday living situations. Her life is devoted to giving and helping others. The light of love, the light of God that shines in Linda, is an inspiration to everyone who meets her.

Linda's story reminds us that we *always* have a choice— whether we want to hear and respond to the voice of God, our true reality, or continue to be imprisoned by the limitations of our ego-mind. And we constantly need to remind ourselves of this. Freedom comes when we know in our hearts that we are one with God and our brothers, and that the love we share is boundless and eternal.

As we meditate on today's lesson, let us review the following thoughts:

Only my condemnation injures me. *Without condemnation I can be free of guilt and fear. If I believe that I can hurt others, I must also believe that they can harm me.*

Today I will claim my own freedom by accepting forgiveness for myself and extending it to everyone, as I remind myself: I choose gladly to release myself and everyone I know from the prison of condemnation.

Steps for Integrating Today's Lesson into Our Daily Life Experiences

1. Quiet your mind. Identify any feelings of frustration, depression, or pain that you may be experiencing today.

2. Then look for any unforgiving thought that may lie beneath your discomfort. Remind yourself that only your condemnation injures you—and only your forgiveness will set you free.

3. Linda Berdeski uses the following criteria to define "apple biting." Ask yourself these questions today:

    Do I criticize others?
    Do I criticize myself?
    Do I condemn others?
    Do I condemn myself?

Do I judge the present by the past?
Does human judgment of good and bad
  govern my thinking?

4. In all situations and encounters today let us remember God's presence within us as we open our minds to this thought from *A Course in Miracles:*

God Himself is incomplete without me.

Remember this when the ego speaks, and you will not hear it. The truth about you is so lofty that nothing unworthy of God is worthy of you. Choose, then, what you want in these terms and accept nothing that you would not offer to God as wholly fitting for Him. You do not want anything else.

*"Look lovingly upon the present,
for it holds the only things
that are forever true."*

LESSON TWELVE

I Will Receive What I Am Giving Now

The law of love does not acknowledge different kinds or degrees of love. It recognizes only one: God's love. God's love is total: it is not limited by time, and no one is excluded from it. It can only join, extend, and expand. The law of love teaches us that giving and receiving occur at the same time, and the more we give, the more we reinforce the reality of love's presence in our lives.

The Law of the World

The principle many of us operate on, however, is quite different. It says if we give to others, we will have less. The law of the world seems to be, "Get as much as you can, and hold on to it. And when things get really tough, always think of yourself first."

This principle of giving, which is based on the perceptions of our ego, convinces us that some people are more
worthy of our love than others, and we can judge this by
how they act and by what our eyes and ears tell us about
them. Indeed, the ego persuades us it is our job to determine which people it is safe to love and which ones it is
not, based on how they appear and act. This basis for giving would also have us believe that there are different
kinds and degrees of love, and it is we who must decide
what kind of love is appropriate to our various relationships.

In a world that believes in a past, present, and future,
giving and receiving cannot occur simultaneously. In the
time-limited world of our ego, giving is usually conditional. This is another way of saying that giving depends
on whether or not the person to whom we have chosen to
give performs in a way we find acceptable.

Unconditional vs. Conditional Love

According to the law of love, giving means that all of
one's love is extended with no expectations. It means the
other person is under no obligation to return our love or to
change in any way. Total giving means unconditional love.

Most of us practice conditional love in our lives—an "I
will love you if . . ." kind of love that depends on the behavior and performance of others. The message we send
out frequently says, "If you fit into the pattern of expectations that I have for you, I will love you." So often what we
really say to others is, "If you could just change this one
thing, then I could love you completely."

Many of us wish our parents could have been different
when we were growing up, and we may still be trying to
change them. We wish they could have expressed their
love for us in a different form—one we would have pre-
ferred. When we get caught up in these thoughts, it can be

helpful to remember that our parents did the best they could for us at the time, based on the circumstances of their own life experiences. No matter how we were brought up, or whether we feel our parents did or did not give us enough love, the truth of the matter is that to receive unconditional love, we must give unconditional love. And this is not only true of our relationships with our parents, but with all our other relationships as well.

The Olympic Jump of Joy

The miracles that can come from unconditional love are dramatically expressed in the following letter I received about a mother whose son competed in the 1984 Winter Olympics.

Dear Jerry,

Since Bob and I last saw you, many exciting things have taken place which we would like to share with you. There is one story especially which I think you might enjoy. Early in February, I had lunch with a woman named Susie Hastings two days before she was heading over to Sarejevo to watch her son, Jeff, compete in the 70 and 90 meter Olympic ski jumping competition.

Her family's life recently had been one of over-whelming media hype because Jeff was a gold medal hopeful for the U.S.A. I think the pressure was getting to all of them. Out of the blue, I had an urgent sense that I needed to tell her about a new book I had just been reading called *Teach Only Love*. It was the one book she took along to read during her stay in Yugoslavia. On the bus ride up the mountain to see her son compete, before she went to bed and over morning coffee she read your book.

Jeff was doing extremely well in the preliminary jumps for the 70-meter competition, placing first on a couple of days. However, during the actual medal jumps he finished ninth. As Jeff told her, "Mom, at the top of the run I felt my turtleneck was too tight." In other words, he had choked.

Next came the practice week for the 90-meter jump and as the week wore on Jeff's jumping got worse and worse. Jeff was concerned, his parents, friends and coach puzzled. This had never happened to Jeff before. He was losing confidence.

Susie continued to read and re-read your book. The night before the 90-meter final competition, Susie and her husband, Paul, went over to Jeff's room and left a note which said, "Take a note from your own book, Jeff, and remember that this is just another World Cup meet. Have fun, fly like a bird and remember that we love you no matter what." Returning to their hotel room to make a large banner for the next day, they found a note which Jeff had left earlier saying, "Better pray hard for me tonight—I really need it." Susie said that in their family, praying means sending love and light and energy; it doesn't mean "winning." However, in all his years of jumping Jeff had never written or said anything like that so she knew he was feeling very discouraged.

All during the time they were making the banner, Susie kept feeling she needed to leave another message for Jeff. So at 12:15 that night she hired a taxi to deliver a second note to Jeff. It said, quite simply, "Remember the good ones."

The next day Jeff's first jump was mediocre and he placed twelfth in the first round. However, when he got to the top for his second and final round, he executed a super jump. He had, indeed, "Remembered the good ones," placing fourth in the Olympics—just 1.7 meters shy of winning the bronze medal. Later, in reference to the notes his mother had sent him on the eve of his jump, Jeff commented, "And where is the jumping fairy when you need her? Right on your shoulder as it turns out?"

Susie told me that the universal message of love, that we are all one and that only our minds limit our potential—the principles contained in *Teach Only Love*—were a constant, reassuring reminder to her whenever she felt tempted to get caught up in the pressure and stress of these highly competitive events. Well, Jerry, the world of love is powerful and it speaks in miraculous ways.

I hope we'll get a chance to see you.

Love,
(signed) *Ann*

Although not all of us can win an Olympic medal, all of us can participate in and experience the rewards of love which we are willing to offer others now.

Geraldine's Gift

The children at our Center for Attitudinal Healing seem to know instinctively that they will receive what they give now, and they demonstrate this regularly. One of the most powerful examples of giving and receiving they have shared with me involved a fourteen-year-old girl named Geraldine who came to our center several years ago.

Geraldine was suffering from a brain tumor and having a lot of trouble getting along with other children.

When I first met Geraldine and her parents, they presented me with a thick file of material, most of which documented her negative, uncontrollable behavior. They were surprised when I said, "Rather than review this file and dwell on Geraldine's past problems, I would like to try another approach. Tell me the positive things you know about Geraldine. Tell me about her strengths rather than her weaknesses." At first, it was hard for her parents to think of anything positive to say, but as they began to focus only on Geraldine's assets, I noticed that their emotions began to shift, and they brightened up considerably.

In addition to the difficulties she had had in interacting with her peers, Geraldine had a complicated medical history, including surgery. She had also undergone chemotherapy, which caused her hair to fall out. As a result of being bald, she had been teased a great deal by other children.

Although Geraldine was very shy and had never talked to children who were experiencing problems similar to hers, she decided to attend one of our children's group meetings. The evening she came, there were several children in the group who were returning to school for the first time after having lost their hair as a result of chemotherapy. They were frightened because they thought they would be the targets of jibes and taunts when their classmates saw their bald heads. As Geraldine listened to them talk about their fears, she suddenly began to open up. In a very helpful way, she shared with them what she had experienced when she faced this situation. She told them what had worked for her in dealing with her classmates' reactions, and what had not; she gave of herself totally. As she radiated love to all of us and allowed herself to accept the love that we extended to her, it became very clear to everyone in that room that giving and receiving were inseparable and instantaneous.

I will never forget what happened when the meeting was over. With tears brimming in her eyes, Geraldine ran up to her parents and said, "I've never experienced so much love from other children ever! Can I come back here?" Learning from Geraldine's example, her parents were able to relax and release, and they began to cry, too. It was as though they had finally come home—"home," of course, being a place where there is unconditional love and where the peace of God can be experienced. Although Geraldine and her parents lived some seventy miles away from Tiburon, she did, in fact, continue to attend our meetings on a regular basis.

A Surprise from St. Francis

A third example of today's lesson has to do with some wooden statues of St. Francis of Assisi carved by the artist Ortega, who has a studio just outside Santa Fe, New Mexico.

About six years ago a friend and I purchased a two-foot statue of the saint for Bill Thetford, and last year I bought a comparable one for my friend, Diane Cirincione. I bought a smaller, ten-inch one for myself to keep on my coffee table as a reminder of the powerful prayer of St. Francis, which I repeat every morning:

Prayer of St. Francis of Assisi

Lord, make me an instrument of thy peace.
Where there is hatred, let me sow love;
Where there is injury, pardon;
Where there is doubt, faith;
Where there is despair, hope;
Where there is darkness, light;
Where there is sadness, joy.

O Divine Master, grant that
I may not so much seek to be
consoled, as to console;
To be understood, as to understand;
To be loved, as to love;
For it is in giving that we receive;
It is in pardoning that we are pardoned; and
It is in dying that we are
born to eternal life.

Since I have been on a spiritual path, I have been doing my best not to be attached to anything I own. As I look back now, however, I realize that of all the things I've owned, I was most attached to that little statue of St. Francis.

Last fall, The Center for Attitudinal Healing held a party at my house to honor our volunteers. Romney Fennell, who was volunteer coordinator as well as the mother of a daughter with leukemia, saw the statue of St. Francis on my table and immediately fell in love with it.

I decided to give it to her on the spot, and as I did I felt a tremendous sense of joy. As the weeks went by, I was surprised to realize that I did not miss the statue at all.

A couple of months ago, Diane and I were invited to give the Sunday sermon at Hugh Prather's "Dispensable Church" in Santa Fe. Imagine what a joyous surprise it was for me to receive at the end of the service—as a present from the congregation—a beautiful four-foot statue of St. Francis carved by Mr. Ortega! The people at the church did not know that I had given my statue away, but they had felt "guided" to present me with this special gift. They certainly taught me that giving and receiving are one and the same.

These examples highlight the importance of expressing unconditional love in our lives. We can remind ourselves of this as we review today's lesson:

I will receive what I am giving now. *Giving and receiving are one and must occur together. I can only receive what I give. This is true in all situations and relationships in my life.*

Steps for Integrating Today's Lesson into Our Daily Life Experiences

1. Upon awakening today say out loud the prayer of St. Francis of Assisi and do your best to apply it in every situation that arises today.

2. Quiet your mind and meditate on the following thought: Since I want to receive peace and love throughout this day, I will say silently or directly to everyone I meet: "I offer you peace and love, and accept love and peace for myself."

3. Imagine a beautiful, still pond of water on a quiet summer day. Drop a pebble in that pond and see how the ripples affect every particle of water. Imagine that these ripples, extending outward to everyone unconditionally, are your thoughts of love.

4. Think of someone you are tempted to want to change. Today, practice letting go of that temptation by repeating to yourself, "*(Specify name)*, I accept you wholly as you are."

5. Remind yourself frequently today that the more love you give, the more you have, as you say to yourself: *I will receive what I am giving now.*

"Attack will always yield to love
if it is brought to love,
not hidden from it."

LESSON THIRTEEN

Forgiveness Offers
Everything I Want*

Can you imagine what it would be like to wake up with no worries or anxieties, no fears, no holding on to guilt feelings or grievances from the past, and no doubts or uncertainties about the future? Can you imagine waking up and feeling perfectly happy, peaceful, and loving? All of this is possible when our forgiveness is complete, since forgiveness offers everything we want.

Celestial Amnesia

What would happen if all of us closed our eyes for just an instant, and totally forgave the world and everything in it—awakening together with only love in our con-

*A Course in Miracles, Workbook, Lesson 122.

sciousness? Imagine this awakening as a rebirthing process in which there would be absolutely no memory of any fear, guilt, or pain you had ever experienced. Let your mind grasp the concept of what Dr. William Thetford calls "celestial amnesia," a state in which the only experience in your memory bank is the love that you have given and received. And this love has no past, present, or future because what we are talking about is God's love, which is changeless and eternal.

God's love is within us, whether our eyes are closed or open, whether we are asleep or awake. It is always there; it has always been there; and it will always be there.

The Light of Love

If you are willing, it is possible to extend the limits of your imagination right now. Begin by sensing how it feels to be lifted up and out of the self-imposed prison of the ego-mind, which makes thoughts of attack, despair, and death seem inevitable. Feel how light you become as you release yourself from the gravity and weight of fear, sin, guilt, and pain. Delight in the sense of freedom that is yours as you find yourself lifted up into a world without judgment and blame, a world where people no longer attack, but simply love one another.

There is nothing to fear because sin, guilt, and pain have no reality here. For just one moment awaken to the truth of who you are and recognize that your only identity is love. Allow yourself to feel the limitless joy and peace of knowing that you are loved forever by God, and that you are joined with Him and all of His creations through love. For the truth is that we are love, and, as such, we are miracle-givers to each other. As explained in Chapter 1, miracles are defined as those shifts in perception that remove the blocks to the awareness of love's presence in our lives.

Awakening

What I have just described does not have to be an imaginary experience. The light of God's love *is* within us now, and we do not have to wait for a "better tomorrow" to experience consistent peace and happiness in our lives today.

The joy of heaven can be ours right now—not as a place, but as a state of oneness, a state of total and perfect joining. All we have to do is be willing to awaken from our sleep and recognize that the waking state we thought we were in is but a dream—a dream of an illusory world in which separation and attack appear to be real.

The Bible tells us, for instance, that Adam was put into a deep sleep from which he never awakened. It would seem that we, like Adam, have been asleep for a long time now, and our awakening, or rebirth, depends on our willingness to let go of the pain, guilt, and fear to which we have been attached. For it is our attachment to pain, guilt, and fear that prevents us from seeing the light of God—our true reality—in our brothers and ourselves.

Releasing the Prison of Our Mind

I would like to share with you a story about a man who came into my life to demonstrate the miracle of love that comes from forgiveness.

Since the publication of my book, *Love Is Letting Go of Fear*, I have become accustomed to receiving many letters of appreciation from people who have found it helpful in their lives. One day, however, I received a letter from a man I shall call Dave. Dave stated that he had just finished *Love Is Letting Go of Fear*, and that it was absolutely the worst book he had ever read. He went on to say that he was in solitary confinement in a high-security prison, and that if I had undergone the kind of treatment and brutality he was receiving from prison guards, I too would be convinced that there are some things people do that are simply unforgivable. He went on to say that I must be some crazy psychiatrist who was living on cloud nine.

I wanted very much to respond to Dave in a way that would be defenseless. I did not want to perceive him as attacking, but rather see him as a desperate man who was feeling a total lack of love in his life and was asking for an expression of love from me. With this in mind, I wrote him a letter, and we began to correspond regularly.

About six months later, I discovered that I was scheduled to lecture in a city some two hours' drive from his prison. I phoned the warden and obtained special permission to see Dave at eight o'clock on Saturday morning. My guidance was to spend that time with him, offering him the love he so desperately needed by accepting him exactly as he was, with no conditions or desire to change him.

Dave came into the waiting room, and we exchanged a quick greeting. Then he took one long breath and began to talk nonstop. His monologue continued for about fifty-five minutes. In almost every sentence he was blaming someone. He certainly demonstrated the ego's belief that if something is wrong in your life, find someone to blame for it.

He blamed his parents for the physical and emotional abuse he had suffered as a child. He blamed his father for being an alcoholic and deserting the family. He blamed his mother for playing musical chairs with men, and for being responsible for his placement in many foster homes and juvenile halls. He blamed society for the fact that he had been in prison for most of his life.

He said he was now serving a sentence for embezzlement, but that he was innocent of these charges. He had not committed this crime; the authorities had arrested the wrong man. He added that because of his poor behavior record in prison, he would not be eligible for parole for at least eight years.

As we were getting close to the end of our hour together, I told him I would have to leave in about five minutes. Then I asked, "Is there anything else you want to say?" He replied, "Yes." He went on to state that he wanted me to send him a television when I got back to California, and he specified that it be a color set, not a black and white one. His reasons for demanding that it be a color set seemed obscure but unequivocal.

As I was leaving, it occurred to me to tell him that I was going to be giving a lecture later that day. I asked him if I could be his mouthpiece what would be the one message he would like me to tell the audience. Without batting an eye he replied, "Tell your audience that to have peace of mind, the most important thing that they could do would be to find people in their lives that they were holding grievances against and forgive them."

Dave's response was an overwhelming surprise to me since it was in total opposition to what he had been saying for the past hour! What a perfect example of how split our minds can be! And what an important reminder to all of us that there is a part of our mind that always knows the truth even when our ego is filled with fear.

Before leaving, I told Dave that at our Center for Attitudinal Healing, we believe nothing is impossible. Rather, it is our thoughts that make up our reality, and what we believe will determine what we see. I suggested that he, too, could change his belief system, that he could see himself as eligible for parole much sooner than his present belief system permitted him to believe was possible.

During my lecture later that day, I shared with the audience the experience I had had with Dave. I mentioned that we heal ourselves as we give ourselves to others. Then it occurred to me to give Dave's prison address to the audience with the suggestion that anyone who would like to write to him could do so. When I returned to California, I sent Dave fifty dollars' worth of postage stamps instead of a color TV.

About five weeks later, I received a letter from Dave, and he said, "Gee, Jerry, there are people outside of prison with worse problems than I have in prison." He went on to say that a large number of people had written asking for help, and he added, "Who am I to try to help anyone when, in fact, I am in solitary confinement and not even able to make it in prison." On the basis of his past, Dave was judging himself as one of the most guilty and unforgivable persons alive.

He did say, however, that in writing to others and trying to help them, he found that he was looking at himself, his parents, and his guards differently. He said he was beginning to think that the cement walls were not his prison, but that he was imprisoned by the guilt and fear in his mind, which he had allowed to immobilize him. And he added that he was seeing the value of forgiveness in releasing him from these negative emotions. A couple of months later, I received a letter from a minister who was a regular visitor of Dave's telling me of the amazing transformation he had observed in Dave.

About a year after our visit, I received a letter from Dave telling me that he was going to appear before the parole board and would like me to write a letter of recommendation for him. I wrote back that I didn't feel I could write a letter of recommendation on the basis of having met with him just once, but I would be glad to write a letter telling the prison officials about our visit and the letters we had exchanged.

Two months later I received a phone call from Dave. He is out of prison now and living with one of the women who had corresponded with him. In trying to help Dave, it had never occurred to me that I might end up as a matchmaker!

Dave's experience illustrates beautifully the theme of today's lesson. It is his personal demonstration of the truth expressed in the following quotation from *A Course in Miracles:**

> **Forgiveness offers everything I want.** *What could you want that forgiveness cannot give? Do you want peace? Forgiveness offers it. Do you want happiness, a quiet mind, certainty of purpose, and a sense of worth and beauty that transcends the world? Do you want care and safety, and the warmth of sure protection always? Do you want quietness that cannot be disturbed, a gentleness that never can be hurt, a deep abiding comfort, and a rest so perfect it can never be upset?*
>
> *All this forgiveness offers you, and more. It sparkles on your eyes as you awake, and gives you joy with which to meet the day. It soothes your forehead while you sleep, and rests upon your eyelids so you see no dreams of fear and evil, malice, and attack. And when you wake again, it offers you another day of happiness and peace. All this forgiveness offers you, and more.*

Steps for Integrating Today's Lesson into Our Daily Life Experiences

1. Ask yourself the following questions:
   a. Do I truly want to be happy?
      Do I truly want to be peaceful?
      Do I truly want to experience love?
      Do I truly want to let go one hundred percent of all my past grievances?
   b. Then think of a specific person in your life—past or present—who you feel is responsible for blocking your awareness of peace and joy.

A Course in Miracles, Workbook, Lesson 122.

   c. Ask yourself if you are truly willing to forgive
that person for what you think he or she may
have done to you. If your answer is "yes," make
a commitment to yourself to begin right now to
see this person differently—through the eyes of
love.

2. Think of an incident—past or present—in which
you felt (or feel) responsible for causing another to
experience pain or suffering.
   a. See the person who comes to mind as completely healed and whole.
   b. Remind yourself that your true mind contains
only thoughts of love. Be willing to forgive
yourself for whatever wrongs you think you
have committed in the past.

3. Repeat to yourself frequently today, "I do not have
to wait for others to accept forgiveness for themselves. I gladly accept forgiveness for myself now."

4. Imagine you have a mammoth key ring with hundreds of keys on it. These are all keys that you have
used to open the door to money, boats, vacations,
special relationships, etc. However, none of them
has brought you the consistent peace and joy you
have been seeking. Visualize yourself throwing all
of those keys away. Now imagine you are surrounded by light, which gradually assumes the
shape of a key in the form of a laser beam. See this
as the key of forgiveness and know that it offers
you everything you want.

5. Now that you have released yourself and others
through forgiveness, allow yourself to experience
the joy and peace of knowing that you are loved
forever by God and are joined with Him and all
others through love.

*"Defenselessness is all that is
required for the truth to dawn
upon our minds with certainty."*

LESSON FOURTEEN

In My Defenselessness
My Safety Lies*

The Cycle of Attack

There is a prevailing belief in the world today that it is not only natural but sensible to be prepared to defend ourselves at all times. We have adopted this attitude because we believe that attack is inevitable, and we need to be ready to strike back when it occurs. According to this way of thinking, the more defensive we are, the less likely it is that someone will attack us. This belief is demonstrated not only in our personal relationships, but in our international relationships with other countries. We have been persuaded by leaders—whose views are supported by a majority of the population—that the more military weapons we accumulate, the stronger we will be. Consequently, it is felt that the mere possession of large numbers of weapons

*A Course in Miracles, Workbook, Lesson 153.

will cause another country to think twice before launching an attack against us. When we are being defensive we are encouraging more attack and forgetting that our function is forgiveness.

We demonstrate defensiveness on a personal level in many ways. The rule of thumb seems to be, "If you perceive someone as attacking you, attack back." For instance, if someone yells at you and you don't feel you've done anything to warrant his anger, yell back at him. Attack! Attack! Attack! Where there is attack, there is no love. You simply cannot attack someone or have attack thoughts and be loving at the same time. Fear and attack thoughts are followed by guilt; and then fear, guilt, anger, attack, and defense become inextricably interwoven.

When we operate according to God's law, the law of love, we recognize the light of love in everyone we see, and our perceptions of attack and defense cease to exist. When we choose not to perceive attack in others or in ourselves, there is no fear and we can experience our natural state of defenselessness.

Illusions without Value

On the contrary, when we find ourselves feeling angry, it is because we still believe that fear and guilt are real. Sometimes we try to suppress or repress our anger only to have it emerge in another form, such as an attack on our own bodies. So suppression and repression of our feelings is not the solution to the problem. The answer lies in recognizing that fear, guilt, and anger themselves are illusions and therefore valueless. When we become aware that something has no value, we are then in a position to let go of it. We only become attached and hang on to that which we value.

We have already discussed the fact that we have but two emotions: love and fear. Love is our natural inheritance, and fear is something our mind invents. Fear cannot be real. It is always an illusion, which comes from our misinterpretation of being attacked, and it is very often accompanied by anger and guilt.

The love of God is the only reality there is, and the thought of love is all that our mind is. Since minds cannot attack—only bodies can do that—the illusion that we are bodies is but the misperception that we are separate from God and each other.

The master teacher, Jesus, taught us many times during his life on this earth that the only thing that has value, the only thing that is real, is love. He knew his only true relationship was with God, and within this relationship there was absolutely no fear. In the security of knowing that his Father would never abandon him or leave him comfortless, Jesus continually demonstrated to us what it means to be defenseless in our relationships with other people.

Last year, I received a letter from Joanne Wilson telling me about her experience in defenselessness. I would like to share it with you.

Dear Dr. Jampolsky,

In rereading the October issue of *Unity* magazine and your article, "In My Defenselessness My Safety Lies," I decided to write to you of an experience I had in defenselessness being my safety.

Last year just before Christmas, I got the afternoon off. Because of the blizzard, my boss didn't think any more customers would be coming in. So I took the opportunity to go Christmas shopping. I had one gift to get in another town forty-three miles away. Since the weather was "bad," I prayed about going, and felt that I was supposed to; so I set out. I felt almost "driven" to go that day.

The roads were terrible, and I felt like turning

back several times, but kept going. I went to the store where I had decided the gift might be, found and bought it quickly, and left.

The traffic leaving town was very slow due to the slippery conditions, and it was almost bumper to bumper, when I noticed a man on the side of the road hitchhiking. The Lord had been instructing me for some time not to be afraid of anything, to get over my fear of picking up hitchhikers, and to replace fear with love. So I did not hesitate to stop and offer this man a ride.

He seemed to hesitate getting into my car—he seemed surprised that a woman stopped for him, particularly a white woman, as he was Indian. But, he got in. He was probably on drugs. At first I thought he was drunk, but there wasn't any alcohol odor. He was very upset and acted sick, and when I asked him where he wanted to go, he said he didn't know. I mentioned a couple of places where I thought he could get help, but he said, "No." He would gaze at me very soberly at times, searching my eyes, and then he would collapse into tears. Leaning forward on his hands, he said over and over, "I don't want to hurt you, I'm sorry." Then he would look at me again—he would seem to "sober up," focus his gaze on me, finger his pocket, and each time, he would start to cry again and completely break down.

We were driving closely behind a large truck, so our visibility was very limited. I did not see the barricade up ahead until I was stopped. There were police cars at the side of the road, and the police were slowing each car, peering inside, and motioning them on. After the truck ahead slowed down and speeded up again, I was surprised to see policemen motioning us to slow down and then stop. The Indian man said to me, "Don't tell them who I am," which he hadn't told me anyway, and then he nonchalantly rolled the window down on his side. The patrolman called him by name, pulled him out of the car, and slapped handcuffs on him so fast, I hardly knew what happened. He motioned me to move on, without questioning me (which surprised me and my husband, when I told him later).

I had been trying to think what I could say to this man as a witness for Christ, when he was so quickly removed from my car, so I blurted out to him, "God go with you, friend," before I drove away.

This man had been completely disarmed by my lack of fear and my concern for him. I'm sure he had a weapon in his pocket and had planned to use it to force someone to help him get away. Instead, he was confused and rendered helpless. The police officer had no trouble apprehending him. He did not struggle, and he was actually calm at the time, even peaceful.

I cried for awhile on the way home, thinking I should have known what to say to help this man who was so troubled and desperate. And then I began to rejoice when I realized that Jesus had meant for me to go there and do just what I did. That the way to help this man at that moment was to stop him from doing something that would hurt someone in his fear and desperation.

The love that Jesus had taught me to replace fear with came through, and even though I was defenseless, I was safe through it all. As you could say, my defenselessness was my safety.

My sincere wish is for your continued success,
(signed) *Joanne Wilson*
P.S. The roads were terrible going home that day, but I rejoiced all the way home and got there fine.

Joanne's account of the power of her defenselessness in a highly charged situation is certainly a dramatic and forceful example of today's lesson. It is also a testament of her willingness to listen to and trust her inner guidance— which is also a demonstration of defenselessness.

"Button-Pushers" as Teachers

One of the benefits of traveling and speaking is that I am frequently challenged to put into practice the concepts I lecture about. These challenges serve as a reminder to me that we always teach what we want to learn.

One such challenge occurred a few years ago while I was on a lecture tour of Australia. During my travels throughout the country, I was invited to make a number of radio and TV appearances. In Sydney, I encountered an interviewer for a radio program who, through the eyes of my ego, appeared to be very hostile. In the interest of anonymity, I shall call him Roger. He began our dialogue by stating that he thought my ideas were shallow, hollow, and without substance. I believe most people would have described his interviewing technique as provoking, attacking, and demeaning.

I must admit, my first reaction was one of fear, and I was tempted to be defensive. Roger "pushed my buttons." However, before saying something that would have caused us both to suffer pain, guilt, and separation, I was able to stop and remind myself that I truly wanted peace of mind. I decided to be defenseless. Rather than seeing Roger as attacking me, I chose to view him as fearful and giving me a call of help for love. For the next several minutes, I concentrated on sending him loving thoughts without any expectation of changing his behavior. It was interesting to note, however, that during the last ten minutes of the interview his remarks seemed to soften quite a bit.

That night I delivered a public lecture. Imagine my

amazement as I gazed out over the audience to see my interviewer of the morning sitting in the third row!

The next day I received a telephone call from Roger. He seemed quite friendly and asked if I would be willing to talk with him about a personal problem, which was causing him considerable conflict. I agreed to do so, and he came up to my hotel room.

Roger seemed altogether different from the man I met at the radio station. He was warm, gentle, and—even more surprising to me—he was trusting. He shared intimate details about himself that I think most people might have been a bit reluctant to mention in an initial interview. It was clear that he felt he was in a safe place with me.

During our discussion, my thoughts went back to the radio interview, and I felt grateful that during it I had been able to be defenseless. My hunch was that most people Roger interacted with attacked him back—and he later confirmed that this was true. The guilt he felt about his own anger was monumental—and I focused on helping him let go of his attraction to guilt. Later he wrote me a letter of appreciation for the help he had received from our discussion.

Before I was on a spiritual pathway, I feel certain that my old personality-self would have been defensive and attacked Roger back during our radio interview. Both of us would then have ended up suffering pain, guilt, and feelings of separation and lack of love.

Roger was a compelling witness to me that when you change your mind, you see a different world. He demonstrated that you *can* choose peace instead of conflict, and love instead of guilt. Once again I learned that we can heal our relationships the moment we say "good-bye to guilt." When we no longer place any value on seeing ourselves as victims or have any investment in being defensive and attacking, we will then experience only love.

Every day we are offered new opportunities to put today's lesson into effect. There is no aspect of our daily lives that would not benefit if we were to let go of our defensiveness and fear of attack, and rest in the security and protection of God's love. My experience continues to confirm that all the conflictual interactions we have with other people, *regardless of their form*, are simply variations on the game of guilt.

In my defenselessness my safety lies. *A defensive response to an "attacking" world will not work, since it increases our own feelings of weakness and vulnerability. Only the fearful believe that defenses protect them, not recognizing that they are caught in an endless chain of attack and defense. Yet defenselessness is strength and cannot be attacked. Today I recognize that defenses cannot protect us, but actually do the opposite of what we want.*

Steps for Integrating Today's Lesson into Our Daily Life Experiences

1. Think of someone who you feel has attacked you in the past and whom you have not forgiven. As you think of this person say to yourself: "*(Specify name)*, I release you and know that we are both safe and surrounded by God's love. I feel serene and confident that nothing can hurt you or me."

2. Remind yourself frequently throughout the day: "Every time I defend myself against someone, I am actually attacking him/her and withdrawing my love from that person and myself."

3. Throughout the day whenever you feel tempted to attack someone, repeat to yourself: "In my defense-

lessness lies my safety and strength. I choose to leave weakness behind today."

4. If you see or hear of anyone who is being attacked today, remember that your purpose is to extend love rather than to identify with either the "aggressor" or the "victim." Tell yourself, "Today is for love, not for fear and attack." Then choose whatever form of love is most appropriate for you to express in the situation.

5. The following is a prescription to prevent you from seeing others as attacking or yourself as defensive: Still your mind and determine what, if any, guilt thoughts you are holding on to. See these thoughts as unwanted, unreal, and having no value. Now release these thoughts. By letting them go, you will not be tempted to project them onto others.

Epilogue

Guilt is the emotion we invented. It is both our jailer and the jail. It keeps our mind imprisoned and enchained in the bondage of self-condemnation and depression. It is the gravity that keeps us pinned to the ground, limited to a physical reality. It forbids us to awaken from our sleep, and in our dream-state we feel separate from God and our brothers and sisters.

Minds that are joined, and recognize they are, can feel no guilt.* When we awaken to this recognition, we can release fears through forgiveness and truly say "good-bye to guilt." With consistent practice we will experience only

THE PRESENCE OF PEACE

THE PRESENCE OF LOVE

THE PRESENCE OF JOY

THE PRESENCE OF GOD

Let us awaken from our dream-state and be witnesses to each other as we place our trust in God, in ourselves, and in one another.

Let us be free.

Let us be limitless.

Let us be whole, healed, and at one.

Let us cross the bridge of forgiveness together, accepting peace for ourselves as we offer it to the world.

A Course in Miracles, Text, p. 489.

ABOUT THE AUTHORS

PATRICIA HOPKINS is the coauthor with Gerald Jampolsky of a series of articles, "To Give Is to Receive," published recently in *Unity* magazine. She has served as acting director, board member, and consultant to The Center for Attitudinal Healing in Tiburon, California, where she lives.

WILLIAM N. THETFORD was a professor of medical psychology in the Department of Psychiatry, College of Physicians and Surgeons, Columbia University, from 1958 to 1981, and the Director of the Psychology Department, Columbia Presbyterian Hospital, New York City, from 1958 to 1978. He is responsible as coscribe with Helen Schucman, Ph.D., for *A Course in Miracles*, which they transcribed over a period of eight years. He has served for five years as a director of The Center for Attitudinal Healing in Tiburon, California, and as consultant, civilian medical specialist in family medicine at the David Grant USAF Medical Center, Travis Air Force Base, California. He lives in Tiburon.